Charles Causley was among the most important British poets of his generation. He lived almost all his life in his native town of Launceston, Cornwall, where he also once worked as a teacher. He published many collections of his work both for adults and children, and won a number of literary awards and prizes including the Kurt Maschler Award and the Signal Poetry Award. In 1958 he became a Fellow of the Royal Society of Literature and was awarded a CBE in 1986.

He died on 4 November 2003, aged 86, and is buried in St Thomas's churchyard, Launceston, only yards from the spot where he was born.

Charles chose and arranged the poems in this collection: they represent over forty years of work, and feature as great a variety of subject, tone and place as any child could wish for.

John Lawrence was born in Hastings, Sussex, in 1933 and educated in Oxford. He studied at Hastings School of Art and then at the Central School of Art and Design, after which he taught at Camberwell School of Art for thirty years.

To illustrate this book, John travelled to Cornwall to meet Charles Causley and to get a feel for his native Launceston. If you look carefully you will find many references to Cornwall and its history and traditions throughout the book.

CHARLES
CAUSLEY

... by John Lawrence

MACMILLAN CHILDREN'S BOOKS

First published 1996 by Macmillan Children's Books

This edition published 2009 by Macmillan Children's Books
an imprint of Pan Macmillan
20 New Wharf Road, London N1 9RR
Associated companies throughout the world
www.panmacmillan.com

ISBN 978-0-330-46411-6

3 5 7 9 8 6 4 2

A CIP catalogue record for this book is available from
the British Library.

Printed and bound by CPI Group (UK) Ltd, Croydon, CR0 4YY

Contents

Great and Small 47

Outsiders and Insiders   **351**

Myth and Fable

Come Out to Play

Freddie Phipps

Freddie Phipps
Liked fish and chips.
Jesse Pinch liked crime.

Woodrow Waters
Liked dollars and quarters.
Paul Small liked a dime.

Sammy Fink
Liked a lemon drink.
Jeremy Jones liked lime.

Mortimer Mills
Liked running down hills.
Jack Jay liked to climb.

Hamilton Hope
Liked water and soap.
Georgie Green liked grime;

But Willy Earls
Liked pretty girls
And had a much better time.

Mrs Malarkey

Mrs Malarkey
(Miss Rooke, that was)
Climbed to the top of a tree
And while she was there
The birds of the air
Kept her company.

Her friends and her family
Fretted and fumed
And did nothing but scold and sneer
But Mrs Malarkey
She smiled and said,
'I'm perfectly happy up here.

'In this beautiful nest
Of sticks and straw
I'm warmer by far than you,
And there's neither rent
Nor rates to pay
And a quite indescribable view.

'A shield from the snow
And the sun and rain
Are the leaves that grow me round.
I feel safer by far
On this green, green spar
Than ever I did on the ground.'

Mrs Malarkey
She covered herself
With feathers of purple and blue.
She flapped a wing
And began to sing
And she whistled and warbled too.

And the birds of the air
Brought seed and grain
And acorns and berries sweet,
And (I must confirm)
The occasional worm
As an extra special treat.

'Mrs Malarkey!
Come you down!'
The people all cried on the street.
But, *Chirrupy, chirrup*
She softly sang,
And, *Tweet, tweet,*
Tweet, tweet, tweet.
Chirrupy, chirrup
(As smooth as syrup)
And, *Tweet, tweet,*
Tweet, tweet, tweet.

When I Was a Boy

When I was a boy
On the Isle of Wight
We all had a bath
On Friday night.
The bath was made
Of Cornish tin
And when one got out
Another got in.
> First there was Jenny
> Then there was Jean,
> Then there was Bessie
> Skinny as a bean,
> Then there was Peter,
> Then there was Paul,
> And I was the very last
> One of all.

When mammy boiled the water
We all felt blue
And we lined up like
A cinema queue.
We never had time
To bob or blush
When she went to work
With the scrubbing brush.
> First there was Jenny, etc.

When I was a boy
On the Isle of Wight
My mammy went to work
Like dynamite:
Soap on the ceiling,
Water on the floor,
Mammy put the kettle on
And boil some more!
      First there was Jenny, etc.

I Saw Charlie Chaplin

I saw Charlie Chaplin
In 1924
Playing golf with a walking-cane
Outside our front door.

His bowler was a size too early,
His trousers were a size too late,
His little moustache said one o'clock,
His boots said twenty-past eight.

He whacked at a potato.
It broke in the bouncing air.
'Never mind, Charlie,' I said to him.
'We've got some to spare.'

I fetched him out a potato.
He leaned on his S-shaped cane.
'Thanks, kid.' He bowed. He shrugged.
I never saw him again.

My father said Charlie Chaplin
Wasn't Charlie at all.
He said it was someone in our town
Going to a Fancy Ball.

He said it couldn't be Charlie.
That it was Carnival Day.
That Charlie never came to our town,
And he lived in the USA.

Not Charlie Chaplin?
You can tell that tale to the cat.
I don't care what my father said.
I know better than that:

For I saw Charlie Chaplin
Outside our front door
Playing golf with a walking-cane.
It was 1924.

I've Never Seen the Milkman

I've never seen the milkman,
His shiny cap or coat.
I've never seen him driving
His all-electric float.

When he comes by the morning's
As black as printers' ink.
I've never heard his footstep
Nor a single bottle clink.

No matter if it's foggy
Or snow is on the ground,
Or rain or hail or half a gale
He always does his round.

I wonder if he's thin or fat
Or fair or dark or bald,
Or short or tall, and most of all
I wonder what he's called?

He goes to bed so early
That not an owl has stirred,
And rises up again before
The earliest early bird.

God bless the faithful milkman,
My hero – and that's flat!
Or perhaps he's a milklady?
(I never thought of that.)

Steam in the Kettle

Steam in the kettle,
Steam in the pan,
Tell me, tell me
If you can,
As through the white air
You boil and blow –
Where do you come from
And where do you go?

Steam from a tower,
Steam from a train,
You smudge the sky
And are gone again.
Up in the air
You straggle and fly,
But when I call
You never reply.

Steam in the iron
And in the machine,
Keep my clothes
Both neat and clean;
But when your work
Is over and done
As frail as a ghost
You're faded and gone.

Steam from the pipe
And smoke from the stack,
Send me a signal
Of white or black.
You float like a feather
Over the green,
And then it's as if
You never had been.

Mist in the meadow
And fume in the street
– One so bitter
And one so sweet –
What will you write
On the page of day
Before you silently
Hurry away?

Mist and fume
And smoke and steam
– Wilder than water
From sea or stream –
Wandering low
And wandering high
On city stone
Or in country sky:

I see your breath
On the window-pane,
Or crossing the clouds
Like an aeroplane,
Sometimes near
And sometimes far –
Tell me, tell me
Who you are!

Fume and mist
And steam and smoke –
You never heard
A word I spoke;
But till the seven seas
Stop their flow
And the wheeling world
Is turned to snow,
I'll ask you what
I want to know:
*Where do you come from
And where do you go?*

D'Arcy Dent

D'Arcy Dent, a man of Kent,
Went to market without a cent.
He chose an apple, he chose a pear,
He chose a comb for his crooked hair,
He chose a fiddle, he chose a flute,
He chose a rose for his Sunday suit,
He chose some pickles, he chose some ham,
He chose a pot of strawberry jam,
He chose a kite to climb the sky.

How many things did D'Arcy buy?

But when it was the time to pay,
D'Arcy Dent he ran away.

Lie-abed, Loafer

Lie-abed, loafer, lazyboots, drone,
The hen-house is open,
The birds all flown.

Layabout, lounger, lubbard, poke,
The cows are eating acorns
Under the oak.

Idler, skiver, ne'er-do-well, doze,
The goat's in the wash-house
Swallowing the clothes.

Loller, lazylegs, clock-watcher, dream,
The cats are in the dairy
At the milk and cream.

Dawdler, do-little, lallygag, leech,
The sheep are a-stray
On the strong sea beach.

Scrimshanker, shirker, slumberer, slouch,
Wake up, rise up
From your couch:

Mammy and daddy are bound to be
Home from market
By half-past three.

Sexton, Ring the Curfew

Sexton, ring the curfew,
Make the tower sway,
Tell all the children
To come from play.

Ring the bell, sexton,
That everyone may know
It's time for the children
To homeward go.

Here comes Betty,
Here comes May,
Here comes Hetty
Been missing all day.

Here comes Lily,
Here comes Lee,
Here comes Billy
With a cut on his knee.

Here comes Abel,
Here comes Hope,
Here comes Mabel
With a skipping rope.

Here comes Zacky,
Here comes Luke,
Here comes Jackie
With his nose in a book.

Here comes Polly,
Here comes Ruth,
Here comes Molly
With an aching tooth.

Here comes Evie,
Here comes Flo,
Here comes Stevie
With a twisted toe.

Here comes Theo,
Here comes Franz,
Here comes Leo
With a hole in his pants.

Here comes Zoë,
Here comes Jane,
And here's little Joey,
Last again.

When I was a child in my hometown of Launceston the curfew bell (a memory of Norman times) was still rung in the parish church tower for five minutes just after 8 p.m.

Family Album

I wish I liked Aunt Leonora
When she draws in her breath with a hiss
And with fingers of ice and a grip like a vice
She gives me a walloping kiss.

I wish I loved Uncle Nathaniel
(The one with the teeth and the snore).
He's really a pain when he tells me *again*
About what he did in the War.

I really don't care for Aunt Millie,
Her bangles and brooches and beads,
Or the gun that she shoots or those ex-army boots
Or the terrible dogs that she breeds.

I simply can't stand Uncle Albert.
Quite frankly, he fills me with dread
When he gives us a tune with a knife, fork and spoon.
(I don't think he's right in the head.)

I wish I loved Hetty and Harry
(Aunt Hilary's horrible twins)
As they lie in their cots giving off lots and lots
Of gurgles and gargles and grins.

As for nieces or nephews or cousins
There seems nothing else one can do
Except sit in a chair and exchange a cold stare
As if we came out of a zoo.

Though they say blood is thicker than water,
I'm not at all certain it's so.
If you think it's the case, kindly write to this space.
It's something I'm anxious to know.

If we only could choose our relations
How happy, I'm certain, we'd be!
And just one thing more: I am perfectly sure
Mine all feel the same about me.

High on the Wall

High on the wall
Where the pennywort grows
Polly Penwarden
Is painting her toes.

One is purple
And two are red
And two are the colour
Of her golden head.

One is blue
And two are green
And the others are the colours
They've always been.

John Tidy

John Tidy's face is birthday-bright,
His hair is tight and trim,
His hands are scrubbed potato white.
(It's not the same with Jim.)

John Tidy comes home cleaner than
When he went out to play,
And as for dirt and dust they seem
To fly the other way.

John Tidy likes to pass the time
By humming of a hymn
Or saying bits of poetry.
(It's not the same with Jim.)

All brushed and sweet from head to feet
John Tidy walks the town.
He's *never* seen on Castle Green
His shirt-tail hanging down.

John Tidy's good, John Tidy's gold
As any cherubim.
(But as for Johnnie's brother, O,
It's not the same with him.)

If ever was a single pair
(The outside and the in)
As might be dock and daisy,
It's John, and Jim the twin.

Why I don't take to brother John
(So smart, so sleek, so slim)
I just can't put my finger on.
(It's not the same with Jim.)

Balloono

Balloono, Balloono,
  What do you bring
Flying from your fingers
  And fifty bits of string?

Is it the sun
  Or is it the moon
Or is it a football
  For Saturday afternoon?

A peach or a melon?
  Tell me, please.
An orange or an apple
  Or a big Dutch cheese?

See them tugging
  In the bright blue air
As if they would wander
  Everywhere!

Come back, Balloono,
  When I draw my pay
And I'll buy them and fly them
  All away.

Miss Pennyluney

Miss Pennyluney went away
Softly down Quarrywell Lane
In the yellow light of an autumn day
And won't be home again.
The gate is locked, the doors are barred
Both at the front and back,
And there's never a single feather of smoke
Comes out at the chimney stack.
No more I'll hear her feed her hens
In frost or rain or shine,
Or call home Tom her tabby cat
Each evening sharp at nine.
No more she'll hand me through the hedge
An apple red as the sun,
Or every Wednesday (when she bakes)
A home-made saffron bun.
Miss Pennyluney went quite alone
As far as I can tell
The day I heard in Quarrywell Lane
The sound of the minute-bell.

But still I watch the window
That's underneath the thatch
Where Miss Pennyluney looked down at me
And over her garden patch,
And where the hen-roost used to be,
And Tom the tab, and the apple tree.

Newlyn Buildings

When we lived in Newlyn Buildings
Half a hundred years ago
Scents and sounds from every quarter
(Sometimes fast and sometimes slow)
Floated through the bricks and mortar.
Though who had the top apartment
No-one ever seemed to know.

On our left, the Widow Whiting
By a curtain fresh as snow
Sat with cotton and with needle
Working at a little treadle
Hard as ever she could go.
Though who had the top apartment
No-one ever seemed to know.

To our right was Catgut Johnson
With a fiddle and a bow,
Sometimes wrong and sometimes right time,
Morning, noon and often night-time
Playing to his tame white crow.
Though who had the top apartment
No-one ever seemed to know.

Underneath lived Annie Fluther,
Family washing all a-blow,
Image of the perfect mother,
Children neat from head to toe
(Six of one and six the other).
Though who had the top apartment
No-one ever seemed to know.

But I heard, in Newlyn Buildings,
Times and seasons long ago,
Overhead each day from dawning,
Through the night from dark to morning,
Footsteps pacing to and fro,
Footsteps old and footsteps new,
To and fro and fro and to.
Though who had the top apartment
No-one ever seemed to know.

The Reverend Sabine Baring-Gould

The Reverend Sabine Baring-Gould,
    Rector (sometime) at Lew,
Once at a Christmas party asked,
    'Whose pretty child are you?'

(The Rector's family was long,
    His memory was poor,
And as to who was who had grown
    Increasingly unsure.)

At this, the infant on the stair
    Most sorrowfully sighed.
'Whose pretty little girl am I?
    Why, *yours*, papa!' she cried.

The Reverend Sabine Baring-Gould (1834–1924) was Rector for 43 years at Lewtrenchard in Devon. He is the author of the hymn 'Onward, Christian Soldiers'.

What Has Happened to Lulu?

What has happened to Lulu, mother?
    What has happened to Lu?
There's nothing in her bed but an old rag-doll
    And by its side a shoe.

Why is her window wide, mother,
    The curtain flapping free,
And only a circle on the dusty shelf
    Where her money-box used to be?

Why do you turn your head, mother,
    And why do the tear-drops fall?
And why do you crumple that note on the fire
    And say it is nothing at all?

I woke to voices late last night,
    I heard an engine roar.
Why do you tell me the things I heard
    Were a dream and nothing more?

I heard somebody cry, mother,
    In anger or in pain,
But now I ask you why, mother,
    You say it was a gust of rain.

Why do you wander about as though
    You don't know what to do?
What has happened to Lulu, mother?
    What has happened to Lu?

I Won't Go Home

I won't go home by the churchyard.
I know I'm sure to see
Wicked Willy Waters
Waiting there for me.

When there's never a light up in the sky
And the dark spreads like the sea
And the tawny owl goes *wick-e-wick*
In the dusky conker tree,

I know that Willy Waters,
Wrapped up in a big white sheet,
Is lying in wait by the churchyard gate
At the end of St Thomas Street.

He's fixed his face with whitewash,
His thumbs and fingers too,
And he'll shriek and he'll squall and he'll jump the wall
And cry out, 'Whoo-hoo-hoo!'

I won't mind ghosts or goblins
Or demons large or small.
They only live in story books
And they're just not real at all,

And I know it's Willy Waters
Wrapped up in his silly sheet –
But why does he make my hair stand up
And my heart to skip a beat?

I won't go home by the churchyard.
I know I'm sure to see
Wicked Willy Waters
Waiting there for me.

Jeremy Peep

Jeremy Peep
When fast asleep
Walks the level
And walks the steep
Eyes tight shut
And face quite pale
His night-shirt billowing
Like a sail.
Down the stairway
And up the street
With nothing at all
Upon his feet.
His arms out straight
In front of his face
He zigs and zags
All over the place.
He never stumbles,
He never slips,
It's as if he could see
With his finger-tips.
'Don't make him open
As much as an eye,'
The neighbours ever so
Softly sigh,
'Or out of his noddle
His wits will fly!
Just turn him about
And watch him head
Straight back home
To his truckle-bed

And sure and slow
He'll get back in
And draw the covers
Up to his chin.'
And the neighbours they tut
About this and that
And say, 'Jeremy, Jeremy,
What were you at
When the moon was up
And the stars were few
And the Town Hall clock
Was striking two?
Have you *any* idea
Where you were last night
When most good people
Were tucked up tight?'
'Such questions you ask!'
Says Jeremy Peep.
'So silly they strike me
All of a heap!
Walking the town
So wild and wan
With nothing at all
But my night-shirt on?
I can't understand
Why you think I should keep
Such curious habits,'
Says Jeremy Peep.
'Where was I all last night?

Asleep.'

Here Comes Tom Clever

Here comes Tom Clever,
Best scholar ever.
                    Don't care, said Jim.

Here comes Sally Heard,
Sings sweet as a bird.
                    Don't care, said Jim.

Here comes Ned Hales,
Makes up tunes and tales.
                    Don't care, said Jim.

Here comes Polly Friend,
Dived off Land's End.
                    Don't care, said Jim.

Here comes Tony Stone,
Carves wood, carves bone.
                    Don't care, said Jim.

Here comes Dolly Bray,
Swam Widemouth[1] Bay.
                    Don't care, said Jim.

[1] pronounced Widmuth

Here comes Jack Fenner,
Caught the Mermaid of Zennor.
                    Don't care, said Jim.

Here comes Jane Stead,
Does sums in her head.
                    Don't care, said Jim.

Here comes Zacky Sharp,
Plays the Jew's harp.
                    Don't care, said Jim.

Here comes Johnnie Fine,
Sank Polmear Mine.
                    Don't care, said Jim.

Here comes Tamsin Fleet,
Cooks a fine treat.
                    Don't care, said Jim.

Here comes Daisy Fife,
Make a good wife.
                    Going home, said Jim.

Pepper and Salt

Pepper and salt his whiskers,
Pepper and salt his hair,
Pepper and salt the three-piece suit
He always likes to wear.

Pepper and salt his muffler,
His hat, and furthermore
Pepper and salt his overcoat
That hangs behind the door.

Pepper and salt his voice is,
Pepper and salt his eye
As he reads out the register
And we pepper and salt reply.

Pepper and salt his singing
When he rises from his chair
And sets to work with a tuning-fork
And a pepper and salty prayer.

He peppers and salts the blackboard
With every kind of sum,
The names of the British Kings and Queens
And the order in which they come.

With a pepper and salty finger
He stabs the maps and charts
And shows us capes and rivers and straits
In home and foreign parts.

Pepper and salt his spectacles,
And it's peppery salty plain
That pepper and salt is his hand of chalk
And pepper and salt his cane.

But silent now the school bell
That Pepper and Salt would sound,
And vanished is the school to which
We came from miles around.

And we who were village children,
Now white of head or hair,
Can never go down the Old School Lane
But Pepper and Salt is there –

Standing in the school-yard
Where weeds and grasses win:
Every day, old Pepper and Salt
Seeing the children in.

The Fiddler's Son

When I was a little lad
I lay within the cradle,
But through the living street I strolled
As soon as I was able.

There I met the King's young daughter,
She, too, walked the street.
'Come in, come in, little son of a fiddler.
Play me a tune sweet.'

It lasted scarcely a quarter of an hour.
The King he saw me singing.
'You rogue, you thief, what is that song
That to my child you're bringing?
In France there is a gallows built
Whereon you'll soon be swinging.'

In but the space of three short days
I had to climb the ladder.
'O give to me my fiddle to play,
For I'll not play hereafter.'

Then bowed I to, then bowed I fro,
On all the four strings telling.
A fine death lament played I,
And the King's tears were falling.

'My daughter is yours, little fiddler's son,
So to your bride come down.
In Austria is a castle built,
And you shall wear the crown.'

Anonymous: translated from the German

By St Thomas Water

By St Thomas Water
Where the river is thin
We looked for a jam-jar
To catch the quick fish in.
Through St Thomas Churchyard
Jessie and I ran
The day we took the jam-pot
Off the dead man.

On the scuffed tombstone
The grey flowers fell,
Cracked was the water,
Silent the shell.
The snake for an emblem
Swirled on the slab,
Across the beach of sky the sun
Crawled like a crab.

'If we walk,' said Jessie,
'Seven times round,
We shall hear a dead man
Speaking underground.'
Round the stone we danced, we sang,
Watched the sun drop,
Laid our heads and listened
At the tomb-top.

Soft as the thunder
At the storm's start
I heard a voice as clear as blood,
Strong as the heart.
But what words were spoken
I can never say,
I shut my fingers round my head,
Drove them away.

'What are those letters, Jessie,
Cut so sharp and trim
All round this holy stone
With earth up to the brim?'
Jessie traced the letters
Black as coffin-lead.
'He is not dead but sleeping,'
Slowly she said.

I looked at Jessie,
Jessie looked at me,
And our eyes in wonder
Grew wide as the sea.
Past the green and bending stones
We fled hand in hand,
Silent through the tongues of grass
To the river strand.

By the creaking cypress
We moved as soft as smoke
For fear all the people
Underneath awoke.
Over all the sleepers
We darted light as snow
In case they opened up their eyes,
Called us from below.

Many a day has faltered
Into many a year
Since the dead awoke and spoke
And we would not hear.
Waiting in the cold grass
Under a crinkled bough,
Quiet stone, cautious stone,
What do you tell me now?

Timothy Winters

Timothy Winters comes to school
With eyes as wide as a football pool,
Ears like bombs and teeth like splinters:
A blitz of a boy is Timothy Winters.

His belly is white, his neck is dark,
And his hair is an exclamation mark.
His clothes are enough to scare a crow
And through his britches the blue winds blow.

When teacher talks he won't hear a word
And he shoots down dead the arithmetic-bird,
He licks the patterns off his plate
And he's not even heard of the Welfare State.

Timothy Winters has bloody feet
And he lives in a house on Suez Street,
He sleeps in a sack on the kitchen floor
And they say there aren't boys like him any more.

Old Man Winters likes his beer
And his missus ran off with a bombardier,
Grandma sits in the grate with a gin
And Timothy's dosed with an aspirin.

The Welfare Worker lies awake
But the law's as tricky as a ten-foot snake,
So Timothy Winters drinks his cup
And slowly goes on growing up.

At Morning Prayers the Master helves[1]
For children less fortunate than ourselves,
And the loudest response in the room is when
Timothy Winters roars 'Amen!'

So come one angel, come on ten:
Timothy Winters says 'Amen
Amen amen amen amen.'
Timothy Winters, Lord.

                                        Amen.

---

[1] dialect word from north Cornwall used to describe the alarmed lowing of cattle (as when a cow is separated from her calf); a desperate, pleading note.

Photograph

She walks among time-beaten stones
One hand upon the rood beam stair
That rises out of sticks and grass
Into a nothingness of air.

Here, where the abbey's great ship struck
And bramble bushes curve and sprout
She stands her granite-sprinkled ground
And stares the speering camera out.

She's dressed for Sunday: finest serge,
The high-necked blouse, a golden pin.
My grandmother: who sewed and scrubbed,
Cleaned out the church, took washing in.

Too soon, my mother said, too soon
The hands were white and washed to bone;
The seven children grown and gone,
And suddenly a life was done.

Today I stand where she once stood
And stranded arch and column sprawl,
Watching where still the ivy streams
In torrents down the abbey wall.

And still the many-noted rooks
About the tree-tops rail and run;
Still, at my feet, the celandine
Opens its gold star to the sun.

Firm as a figurehead she stands,
Sees with unsparing eye the thread
Of broken words within my hand
And will not turn away her head.

Great and Small

A Leap of Leopards

A leap of leopards,
A sleuth of bears,
A clamour of rooks,
A husk of hares.
> *'Knawed that a'ready,' said Jacker.*
> *'No you never,' said Jan.*

A muster of peacocks,
A team of ducks,
A murder of crows,
A leash of bucks.
> *'Knawed that a'ready,' said Jacker.*
> *'No you never,' said Jan.*

A wing of plovers,
A sounder of swine,
A herd of curlews,
A drove of kine.
> *'Knawed that a'ready,' said Jacker.*
> *'No you never,' said Jan.*

A watch of nightingales,
A pod of seals,
A nye of pheasants,
A spring of teals.
> *'Knawed that a'ready,' said Jacker.*
> *'No you never,' said Jan.*

A chattering of choughs,
A bevy of quails,
A fall of woodcock,
A gam of whales.
>   *'Knawed that a'ready,' said Jacker.*
>   *'No you never,' said Jan.*

The Song of Kruger the Cat

I really hate the coal-man.
I hate his hood and sack.
I'm sure one day he'll carry me off
In a bundle on his back.

When he crunches up to the bunker
And I hear the coal go *crump*
My legs turn into custard
And my heart begins to bump.

I'm not afraid of a bulldog,
A gull or a giant rat,
The milkman or the postman,
Or the plumber, come to that.

But when I hear the coal-man
I shake and quake with fright,
And I'm up and away for the rest of the day
And sometimes half the night.

I'm certain that to his family
He's loving and good and kind,
But when I hear his hobnailed boots
I go right out of my mind.

'Now Kruger, dear,' they say, 'look here:
Isn't it rather droll?
You love to sleep and snore before
A fire that's made of coal.'

But I can't help my feelings
However hard I try.
I really hate the coal-man.
Who's that? Good grief! Good-bye!

A Fox Came into my Garden

A fox came into my garden.
'What do you want from me?'
'Heigh-ho, Johnnie-boy,
A chicken for my tea.'

'Oh no, you beggar, and never, you thief,
My chicken you must leave,
That she may run and she may fly
From now to Christmas Eve.'

'What are you eating, Johnnie-boy,
Between two slices of bread?'
'I'm eating a piece of chicken-breast
And it's honey-sweet,' I said.

'Heigh-ho, you diddling man,
I thought that was what I could smell.
What, some for you and none for me?
Give us a piece as well!'

Good Morning, Mr Croco-doco-dile

Good morning, Mr Croco-doco-dile,
And how are you today?
I like to see you croco-smoco-smile
In your croco-woco-way.

From the tip of your beautiful croco-toco-tail
To your croco-hoco-head
You seem to me so croco-stoco-still
As if you're croco-doco-dead.

Perhaps if I touch your croco-cloco-claw
Or your croco-snoco-snout,
Or get up close to your croco-joco-jaw
I shall very soon find out.

But suddenly I croco-soco-see
In your croco-oco-eye
A curious kind of croco-gloco-gleam,
So I just don't think I'll try.

Forgive me, Mr Croco-doco-dile
But it's time I was away.
Let's talk a little croco-woco-while
Another croco-doco-day.

Aireymouse

Aireymouse, wary mouse,
Steering and veering
At sunrise and sunfall
By tower and tree,
Is it because
You appear to be *peering*
The old wives all said
That you never could see?

Flying mouse, skying mouse,
Neatly and featly,
Skilfully, sweetly
You dive and you dare,
But who was the noddy
Who told everybody
That if you came near
You would lodge in my hair?

Swooping mouse, looping mouse,
Curving and swerving,
Here-ing and there-ing
Now low, now high,
Soft in your silky coat
Through the wild air you float:
Aireymouse, wary mouse
Passing me by
Tell me, O tell me,
Who taught you to fly?

Aireymouse is the country name for a bat; in this case, the pipistrelle.

Python on Piccolo

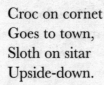

Python on piccolo,
Dingo on drums,
Gannet on gee-tar[1]
Sits and strums.

Croc on cornet
Goes to town,
Sloth on sitar
Upside-down.

Toad on tuba
Sweet and strong,
Crane on clarinet,
Goat on gong.
   And the sun jumped up in the morning.

Toucan travelling
On trombone,
Zebra zapping
On xylophone.

Beaver on bugle
Late and soon,
Boa constrictor
On bassoon.

[1] guitar

Tiger on trumpet
Blows a storm,
Flying fox
On flügelhorn.
  And the sun jumped up in the morning.

Frog on fiddle,
Hippo on harp,
Owl on oboe
Flat and sharp.

Viper on vibes
Soft and low,
Pelican
On pi-a-no.

Dromedary
On double-bass,
Cheetah on 'cello
Giving chase.
  And the sun jumped up in the morning.

The Owl Looked Out of the Ivy Bush

The owl looked out of the ivy bush
And he solemnly said, said he,
'If you want to live an owlish life
Be sure you are not like me.

'When the sun goes down and the moon comes up
And the sky turns navy blue,
I'm certain to go tu-whoo tu-whit
Instead of tu-whit tu-whoo.

'And even then nine times out of ten
(And it's absolutely true)
I somehow go out of my owlish mind
With a whit-tu whoo-tu too.

'There's nothing in water,' said the owl,
'In air or on the ground
With a kindly word for the sort of bird
That sings the wrong way round.

'I might,' wept the owl in the ivy bush,
'Be just as well buried and dead.
You can bet your boots no one gives two hoots!'
'Do I, friend my,' I said.

I Had a Little Cat

I had a little cat called Tim Tom Tay,
I took him to town on market day,
I combed his whiskers, I brushed his tail,
I wrote on a label, 'Cat for Sale.
Knows how to deal with rats and mice.
Two pounds fifty. Bargain price.'

But when the people came to buy
I saw such a look in Tim Tom's eye
That it was clear as clear could be
I couldn't sell Tim for a fortune's fee.
I was shamed and sorry, I'll tell you plain,
And I took home Tim Tom Tay again.

John Clark

John Clark sat in the park,
Saw the sun jump out of the dark,
Counted one and counted two,
Watched the sky from black to blue,
Counted three and counted four,
Heard a horse and then some more,
Counted five and counted six,
Heard a snapping in the sticks,
Counted seven and counted eight,
Saw a fox and saw his mate,
Counted nine and counted ten.

'Hurry home to your den, your den,
Or you never may see the sun again
For I fear I hear the hunting men,
The hunting men and the hounds that bark!'

Said John Clark as he sat in the park.

Spin Me a Web, Spider

Spin me a web, spider,
Across the window-pane
For I shall never break it
And make you start again.

Cast your net of silver
As soon as it is spun,
And hang it with the morning dew
That glitters in the sun.

It's strung with pearls and diamonds,
The finest ever seen,
Fit for any royal King
Or any royal Queen.

Would you, could you, bring it down
In the dust to lie?
Any day of the week, my dear,
Said the nimble fly.

Zow-bug

Zow-bug, zow-bug
Under the stone,
One of a hundred
Or one on your own,
Hurrying, flurrying
To and fro,
Fourteen legs
On the go, go, go,
Why are you hiding
Out of the light?
> *Waiting for day*
> *To turn to night.*

Zow-bug, zow-bug
Scurrying through
A world of dusk
And a world of dew,
Now that you've left
Your house of wood
Is it bad you are up to
Or is it good
Down in the garden
Dark and deep?
> *Taking a turn*
> *Round the compost heap.*

Zow-bug, zow-bug
By the long shore
Tell me who
You are waiting for:
Is it King Neptune,
A sole or a dab,
A Cornish pilchard
Or an ocean crab?
Who will you meet
On Newlyn Quay?

> *My great-great-grandaddy*
> *Lives in the sea.*

Zow-bug (sow-bug) is the country name for the woodlouse, a land-living crustacean distantly related to the crab.

My Cat Plumduff

My cat Plumduff
When feeling gruff
Was terribly fond
Of taking snuff,
And his favourite spot
For a sniff and a sneeze
Was a nest at the very
Top of the trees.

And there he'd sit
And sneeze and sniff
With the aid of a gentleman's
Handkerchief;
And he'd look on the world
With a lordly air
As if he was master
Of everything there.

Cried the passers-by,
'Just look at that!
He thinks he's a bird,
That silly old cat!'
But my cat Plumduff
Was heard to say,
'How curious people
Are today!'

'Do I think I'm a bird?'
Said my cat Plumduff.
'All smothered in fur
And this whiskery stuff,
With my swishy tail
And my teeth so sharp
And my guinea-gold eyes
That shine in the dark?

'Aren't they peculiar
People – and how!
Whoever has heard
Of a bird with a miaow?
Such ignorant creatures!
What nonsense and stuff!
No wonder I'm grumpy,'
Said my cat Plumduff.

The Elephant and the Butterfly

Said the elephant to the butterfly
As they wandered the forest through,
'I wish I could rise up into the skies
And flutter about like you!
If I was as fine as a feather
I'd ramble the wide air round.
It's a terrible bore to never get more
Than a couple of feet off the ground!'

Said the butterfly to the elephant,
'My dear, that sounds perfectly fine.
You could make yourself wings out of palms and things
With the aid of the creeper and vine.
If you turn your trunk like a propeller
In a bit of a following breeze
There's no reason why you won't take to the sky
With simply incredible ease.'

Believe it or not, but no sooner
Had the butterfly uttered these words
Than the elephant flew straight up in the blue
As though he was one of the birds.
High over the trees of the jungle
And high above mountain and scree
The elephant wobbled and wavered
Over land and then over the sea.

'Good gracious!' he cried, and, 'Good heavens!
I'm dizzy from toe to my crown,
And my memory's bad (and isn't it sad?)
But when things go up they come down.
My head it is rolling and reeling
And my stomach has gone on the spree.
I've a notion that if I don't land in the ocean
It's curtains for certain for me!'

But the lucky old elephant landed
In the softest of sea and of sand
And he paddled ashore with a bit of a roar
And sat himself down on the land.
He lifted his voice to the hill-tops
With an elephant trumpet-y sound.
'Do you think, butterfly, I was foolish to try?'
But the creature was nowhere around.

And ever since then you will find him
(That is, if you're anxious to look)
Reclining and reading an encyclopaedian
Sort of a Reference Book.
He studies it morning and evening
(Now and then gazing up in the sky)
On 'How Best to Sight the Butterfly (White)'

And a faraway look in his eye.

Ring Dove

Ring dove, ring dove,
High in the tree,
What are the words
You say to me?

What do you sing
And what do you tell
Loud as the ring
Of a telephone bell?

Take two cows, Davy,
Take them to the shore,
And when you've taken two
Take two cows more.

Tell Me the Time

'Tell me the time,' the wok-wok sang
Flying the China Sea.
'Ten to eleven? Don't say that!
I thought it was half-past three.'

'Tell me the day,' the tyg-tyg called
From the Great Australian Bight.
'Monday morning? Gracious me!
It feels like Saturday night.'

'Tell me the date,' the tass-tass cried
As it circled above Rangoon.
'First of March? According to me
It's the twenty-fourth of June.'

'Tell me the year,' the cran-cran sighed
Swimming by Timbuktu.
'1999? I'm sure
It's 1802.'

And with a small frown each went the same way
The seconds and years had gone.
There really was no more to say,
And the great globe rolled on.

Kensey

Here's a card from Tangier, Kensey.
White African air.
Writing on the back says,
'Wish you were here'.

Here's a card from Kashmir, Kensey.
Fretwork mountain, snow.
Writing on the back says,
'Get up and go'.

Here's a card from Eilat, Kensey.
Snorkels, blue glass bay.
Writing on the back says,
'Sun shines all day'.

Here's a card from Rome, Kensey.
The Spanish Steps, flowers.
Writing on the back says,
'Window marked x = ours'.

Tangier, Kashmir, Kensey,
Eilat and Rome.
What say I stir myself?
Stir the fire instead, mister,
Says my old cat Kensey.
Best stay at home.

I Saw a Jolly Hunter

I saw a jolly hunter
    With a jolly gun
Walking in the country
    In the jolly sun.

In the jolly meadow
    Sat a jolly hare.
Saw the jolly hunter.
    Took jolly care.

Hunter jolly eager –
    Sight of jolly prey.
Forgot gun pointing
    Wrong jolly way.

Jolly hunter jolly head
    Over heels gone.
Jolly old safety-catch
    Not jolly on.

Bang went the jolly gun.
    Hunter jolly dead.
Jolly hare got clean away.
    Jolly good, I said.

Mawgan Porth

Mawgan Porth
The Siamese cat
Lives in an elegant
London flat
Dines on salmon
Sleeps on silk
Drinks Malvern water
Instead of milk
Shops at Harrods
Fortnum & Mason
Has room after room
To run and race in
Wears winter jackets
Of Harris tweed
Strolls in the park
At the end of a lead
But in case you think
As think you might
He's a bit of a drone
Or a parasite
I can tell you quite
Without a qualm
He's a perfectly wonderful
Burglar alarm
For if anyone moves
A bolt or catch

Or touches a single
Security latch
Or worst of all
(I'm certain sure)
Tries to pick the lock
On the big front door
You'll hear him skirl
And you'll hear him squeal
As if his lungs
Were made of steel
You'll hear such a bellow
You'll hear such a blare
As stops the traffic
In Belgrave Square
And for hours and hours
He screeches and squalls
Enough to crack
The dome of St Paul's
Don't you think, I said
To Mawgan Porth
(In his chair that dates
From William IV)
You're a lucky old cat
In this world of strife
To lead such a super-
Superior life?

But nothing he said
As if nothing he knew
Just kept me clearly
Under review
And fixed me firm
With his eyes of blue
His Siamese cat-ical
Aristocratical
Eyes as he gazed me
Through and through.

Dartford Warbler

Stay-at-home
  Never-roam
    Dartford warbler
Hiding in furze
  On the yellow plain,
    Skulking in scrub,
Secret in heather
  As seasons turn
    And turn again;

Spending your day
  On the highest spray
    Or sprig or twig
Where you first
  Saw day;
    Wearing the English
Storm and summer,
  Never, ever
    To fly away.

Restless, hole-in-
   The-corner creeper,
      I watch in spring
When you bob
   Like a ball
      High on the bush-top
Singing, scattering
   Rattling music
      Over all.

Slate-wing, starveling
   Beyond my window,
      Cheery, unweary
In sun, in snow,
   Packed my bag
      I hear you crying,
'*You too! You too!*
   Tell me, spell me
      Why do you go?'

Turnstone

Turnstone, tangle picker,
Sifting the ocean,
Wading the water,
Tipping the stone,
Always you stand
At the brink of the billows,
Neither in deep
Nor on the high strand.

'What is your story?'
I asked of the turnstone
Careful, aware-ful
Between sea and shore;
But all that I heard
Was a chuckle, a twitter,
Nor deep, nor high,
Nothing less, nothing more.

Rocco

I am St Roche's dog. We stand
Together on the painted wall:
His hat tricked with a cockleshell,
Wallet and staff in pilgrim hand.
He lifts a torn robe to display
The plague-spot. I sit up and wait.
A lot of us has peeled away.
My breed is indeterminate.
                    Bow! Wow!

Under a Piacenza sun
The sickness struck him like a flame.
'Dear Lord,' he cried, 'my life is done!'
And to a summer forest came.
But I, his creature, sought him high
And sought him low on his green bed
Where he had lain him down to die.
I licked his wounds and brought him bread.
                    Bow ! Wow!

And he was healed, and to his house
Sick by the hundred seethed and swarmed
As, by God's grace, the Saint performed
Cures that were quite miraculous.
Now my good master's home is where
Are heavenly joys, which some declare
No fish nor bird nor beast may share.
Ask: Do I find this hard to bear?
        Bow! Wow!

The fourteenth-century St Roche, born in Montpellier, was the patron saint
of those suffering from the plague. He spent a great part of his life on pil-
grimages. While ministering to the sick in Italy, he himself caught the plague
in the town of Piacenza. Desperately ill, he retired to the woods to die. A
story tells that here he was discovered by a dog who licked his wounds and
each day brought him a fresh loaf of bread. In early paintings, St Roche is
usually shown wearing a cockleshell (the badge of the pilgrim) in his hat,
and is accompanied by his faithful dog. In the church of St Thomas-the-
Apostle (where I was christened) at Launceston in Cornwall is a faded
medieval wall painting of St Roche and his dog.

For a Moment Rare

For a moment rare
They looked at it there
With its antique glance
And its three-pronged stance,
And from hill to hill
All the folk stood still
As the trino vast
From the living past
Seemed to stare
   And glare
     And leer
       And peer
         And glint
           And squint
   Both here and there
From its crystal lair.

Though its head not a mite
   Moved to left nor right,

Its eye seemed to follow you
Everywhere
With expression strange
That seemed to change
With the shifting
Drifting
Light of day.

And it looked at them all
As if to say,
'Good afternoon –
I'm yesterday.'

From The Tail of the Trinosaur

I Saw a Saw-doctor

I saw a saw-doctor
Down by the saw-mill.
He said, 'I shall stay here,
Young fellow, until
With the aid of this saw-fly,
This rod and this line,
I catch me a saw-fish
        On which I might dine.'

'Come sit on this saw-grass,'
The saw-doctor said,
'And hear the saw-sharpener
Cry overhead.'
But before I could join him,
Could speak or could say,
He sprang on his saw-horse
        And galloped away.

The saw-sharpener is the country name for the great titmouse, with its
metallic two-note call in spring.

One Day at a Perranporth Pet-shop

One day at a Perranporth pet-shop
  On a rather wild morning in June,
A lady from Par bought a budgerigar
  And she sang to a curious tune:
'Say that you love me, my sweetheart,
  My darling, my dovey, my pride,
My very own jewel, my dear one!'
  'Oh lumme,' the budgie replied.

'I'll feed you entirely on cream-cakes
  And doughnuts all smothered in jam,
And puddings and pies of incredible size,
  And peaches and melons and ham.
And you shall drink whiskies and sodas,
  For comfort your cage shall be famed.
You shall sleep in a bed lined with satin.'
  'Oh crikey!' the budgie exclaimed.

But the lady appeared not to hear him
  For she showed neither sorrow nor rage,
As with common-sense tardy and action foolhardy
  She opened the door of his cage.
'Come perch on my finger, my honey,
  To show you are mine, O my sweet!' –
Whereupon the poor fowl with a shriek and a howl
  Took off like a jet down the street.

And high he flew up above Cornwall
    To ensure his escape was no failure,
Then his speed he increased and he flew south and east
    To his ancestral home in Australia,
For although to the folk of that country
    The word 'budgerigar' means 'good food',
He said, 'I declare I'll feel much safer there
    Than in Bodmin or Bugle or Bude.'

ENVOI

And I'm sure with the budgie's conclusion
    You all will agree without fail:
Best eat frugal and free in a far-distant tree
    Than down all the wrong diet in jail.

Moor-hens

Living by Bate's Pond, they
(Each spring and summer day)
Watched among reed and frond
The moor-hens prank and play.

Watched them dip and dive,
Watched them pass, re-pass,
Sputtering over the water
As if it were made of glass.

Watched them gallop the mud
Bobbing a tail, a head;
Under an April stream
Swimming with tails outspread.

Listened at night for a cry
Striking the sky like a stone;
The *kik! kik! kik!* of farewell
As they drifted south for the sun.

Whose are the children, and who
Are the children who lived by the pond,
Summer and spring year-long
When the wild sun shone?
Thirsty the stream, and dry;
Ah, and the house is gone.

My Mother Saw a Dancing Bear

My mother saw a dancing bear
By the schoolyard, a day in June.
The keeper stood with chain and bar
And whistle-pipe, and played a tune.

And bruin lifted up its head
And lifted up its dusty feet,
And all the children laughed to see
It caper in the summer heat.

They watched as for the Queen it died.
They watched it march. They watched it halt.
They heard the keeper as he cried,
'Now, roly-poly!' 'Somersault!'

And then, my mother said, there came
The keeper with a begging-cup,
The bear with burning coat of fur,
Shaming the laughter to a stop.

They paid a penny for the dance,
But what they saw was not the show;
Only, in bruin's aching eyes,
Far-distant forests, and the snow.

Rock Ape

I have climbed a Pillar of Hercules,
A rock swimming in the Middle Sea
And named for the Moorish conqueror
Gebal-al-Tarik.

Below me, beyond the smoking cork woods
Of San Roque, the Phoenicians sailed for tin
To the dark north, the dragon-guarded
Hesperides Garden and its bright apples,
And the surly prophet Jonah was hurled ashore
By a large fish.

In all Europe is no wild tribe such as mine.
I must ask you not to address me as Monkey.
My tall house is of soft grey limestone.
In my falling garden grow
Scarlet geranium, heliotrope, daphne,
The castor-oil plant and a little
Maidenhair fern.

My day is punctuated by the bugle,
Sometimes by a weeping fog from the east,
Sometimes by a snow-cold north wind
From the Serrania de Ronda.

I have seen many sieges,
Heard many speeches
In strange clacking tongues.
All say, 'I want. I want.'

On a glass-clear day I spy
The snow-jagged peaks of the Sierra Nevada
Across the oil-smooth Bay,
In Africa.

Some declare I was brought
By the dark-voiced, fierce and holy
Fathers of the Moriscos;
Others, that I came beneath the waters
Of the strait by a secret path
Known only to my tribe.
I shall not tell you what I know
Of this.

Only that I am marooned here
Since the earth broke apart,
Since the shaking of land and sea
A million days and nights
Ago. And that there will come a time
When sea and land shatter again
And I shall return to the great Sierra,
The cool snows of Africa.

The huge rocks called the Pillars of Hercules guard the western entrance
to the Mediterranean (or Middle) Sea. One is Gibraltar; on the other stands
the town of Ceuta in North Africa. Gibraltar (Gebal-al-Tarik, the Hill of
Tarik) takes its name from Tarik, the Moorish leader who fortified it in AD
711. It is a part of the world rich in myth and fable. One legend tells of how
the famous Barbary apes who live on Gibraltar originally came to the Rock
from Africa by means of a secret tunnel under the sea.

Lion

That's Saint Jerome, my master, over there
Writing a book in Latin. All of five
Years he's been at it. The two of us share
A lodging in this shabby desert cave.

Most folk find him a bit cantankerous.
Tongue like a knife. Gets in an awful tear
With scholars, pilgrims seeking his advice
And (worst of all) tourists who come to stare.

But here I must make one thing very plain:
This wise man has a heart as well as head.
Long years ago he eased a giant thorn
Out of my paw, while other people fled.

He watched, he tended me, quite unafraid,
Till once again I could both race and run,
And then it was a serious vow I made:
I would protect him till my life was done.

I've surely got my work cut out. But then,
I sleep with open eyes, as you will see
In paintings of us by quite famous men,
Although at first you may not notice me.

Sometimes he beats his breast with a flat stone.
Sometimes he gives a very little groan.
(I can't think why.) Well, be that as it may,
To all who call on him from near, from far:
Treat this great scholar with respect, I say.
                    Grrrrrr!

Saint Jerome lived from about 342 to 420 AD. He translated most of the
Bible from its original languages into Latin.

   In earlier times the lion was thought to sleep with its eyes open and so to
be at all times watchful and alert.

Charm and Flower

Spell

When I was walking by Tamar stream
The day was sweet as honey and cream.
The air was brisk as a marriage bell.
(Kiss if you must, but never tell.)

When I was walking by Tamar flood
I plucked a rose the colour of blood.
The red ran out and the thorn ran in.
(Finish all, if you begin.)

When I was walking by Tamar brook
I met a man with a reaping hook.
The beard he wore was white as the may.
(The hours they run like water away.)

When I was walking by Tamar race
I met a maid with a smiling face.
Out of her eyes fell tears like rain.
(You will never see this road again.)

When I was walking by Tamar lock
I picked a bunch of sorrel and dock,
Creeping Jenny and hart's-tongue fern.
(Days they go, but cannot return.)

When I was walking by Tamar spring
I found me a stone and a plain gold ring.
I stared at the sun, I stared at my shoes.
(Which do you choose? Which do you choose?)

In My Garden

In my garden
Grows a tree
Dances day
And night for me,
Four in a bar
Or sometimes three
To music secret
As can be.

Nightly to
Its hidden tune
I watch it move
Against the moon,
Dancing to
A silent sound,
One foot planted
In the ground.

Dancing tree,
When may I hear
Day or night
Your music clear?
What the note
And what the song
That you sing
The seasons long?

It is written
Said the tree,
On the pages
Of the sea;
It is there
At every hand
On the pages
Of the land;

Whether waking
Or in dream:
Voice of meadow-grass
And stream,
And out of
The ringing air
Voice of sun
And moon and star.

It is there
For all to know
As tides shall turn
And wildflowers grow;
There for you
And there for me,
Said the glancing
Dancing tree.

Stone in the Water

Stone in the water,
Stone on the sand,
Whom shall I marry
When I get to land?

Will he be handsome
Or will he be plain,
Strong as the sun
Or rich as the rain?

Will he be dark
Or will he be fair,
And what will be the colour
That shines in his hair?

Will he come late
Or will he come soon,
At morning or midnight
Or afternoon?

What will he say
Or what will he sing,
And will he be holding
A plain gold ring?

Stone in the water
Still and small,
Tell me if he comes,
Or comes not at all.

Foxglove

Foxglove purple,
Foxglove white,
Fit for a lady
By day or night.

Foxglove bring
To friend and stranger
A witches' thimble
For the finger.

Foxglove on
The sailing sea,
Storm and tempest
There shall be.

Foxglove sleeping
Under the sky,
Watch the midnight
With one eye.

Foxglove burning
In the sun,
Ring your bells
And my day is done.

Houseleek

Houseleek, houseleek
On the roof-tree
Send away thunder
To the far sea;
Send away lightning,
Send away storm,
Keep all who live here
Free from harm.

Who plants the sengreen,
Jupiter's Beard,
May of witch and wizard
Never have fear.
'Houselick, houselick,'
My grannie would say,
'Lean on my roof-top
Night and day.

'This way, that way
Lean to me,
Welcome-home-husband-
However-drunk-you-be.
Lean in moonlight,
Lean in sun.
Is one drunken husband
Better than none?'

One of the country names for the houseleek or sengreen (a plant once
thought to have special magical properties) is 'Welcome-home-husband-
however-drunk-you-be'.

Mistletoe

Mistletoe new,
Mistletoe old,
Cut it down
With a knife of gold.

Mistletoe green,
Mistletoe milk,
Let it fall
On a scarf of silk.

Mistletoe from
The Christmas oak,
Keep my house
From lightning stroke.

Guard from thunder
My roof-tree
And any evil
That there be.

At Linkinhorne

At Linkinhorne[1]
Where the devil was born
I met old Mollie Magee.
'Come in,' she said
With a wag of her head,
'For a cup of camomile tea.'
And while the water whistled and winked
I gazed about the gloom
At all the treasures Mollie Magee
Had up and down the room.

With a sort of a smile
A crocodile
Swam under an oaken beam,
And from tail to jaw
It was stuffed with straw
And its eye had an emerald gleam.
In the farthest corner a grandfather clock
Gave a watery tick and a tock
As it told the date and season and state
Of the tide at Falmouth Dock.

[1] village in south-east Cornwall. The first two lines of the poem are a well-known local saying.

She'd a fire of peat
That smelled as sweet
As the wind from the moorland high,
And through the smoke
Of the chimney broke
A silver square of sky.
On the mantelshelf a pair of dogs
Gave a china smile and a frown,
And through the bottle-glass pane there stood
The church tower upside-down.

She'd shelves of books,
And hanging on hooks
Were herbals all to hand,
And shells and stones
And animal bones
And bottles of coloured sand.
And sharp I saw the scritch-owl stare
From underneath the thatch
As Matt her cat came through the door
With never a lifted latch.

At Linkinhorne
Where I was born
I met old Mollie Magee.
She told me this,
She told me that
About my family-tree.
And oh she skipped and ah she danced
And laughed and sang did we,
For Mollie Magee's the finest mother
Was ever given to me.

Hazel

Hazel fork
From hazel tree
Tell me where
The waters be.

Hazel shoot
In my hand
Bring me where
My true-love stands.

Hazel stem,
Hazel leaf,
Show me robber,
Show me thief.

Hazel twig,
Hazel bud,
Keep my house
From fire and flood.

Hazel stick,
Hazel wand,
Save me from
A salt-sea end.

Hazel bush,
Hazel tree,
May you ever
Dwell by me.

Don't Let Baby

Don't let baby look in the mirror,
Don't let baby look in the glass
Lest its life be sad and sorry,
Lest its eyes go bent and boss.
Don't let baby look in the glass
Never until twelve months are past.

Cover up the glass with linen,
Turn it, turn it backsyvore.[1]
Don't let baby look in the mirror
Lest its life be wisht[2] and worried,
Lest it fret and lest it roar
Half its days and then some more.

In earlier times it was believed to be unlucky for a baby to see its reflection
in a mirror or polished surface.
[1] back to front
[2] pale, wan

Dandelion

Dandelion,
Yellow crown,
Now your petals
All are gone,
Speak to me
The time of day
As I blow
Your seeds away.

If at one breath
They are flown
I need never
Hurry home,
But if any
Seeds remain
I must to
My home again.

Dandelion,
Yellow head,
Tell me when
I shall be wed.
Country clock
Without a chime
When shall be
My wedding time?

Dandelion,
Tell me fair
How many children
I shall bear,
Or tell me true
As moon or sun
If there shall be
Never a one.

Dandelion,
Flowering clear
Through the seasons
Of the year
Teach me simple,
Teach me slow
All these things
That I must know.

Tell, Tell the Bees

Tell, tell the bees,
The bees in the hive,
That Jenny Green is gone away,
Or nothing will thrive.

There'll be no honey
And there'll be no comb
If you don't tell the bees
That Jenny's not home.

Tap on their window,
Tap on their door,
Tell them they'll never see
Jenny Green more.

Tell them as true
As you know how
Who is their master
Or mistress now.

Tell all the hives
As they buzz and hum,
Jenny is gone
But another will come.

Tell, tell the bees,
The bees in the hive,
That Jenny Green is gone away,
Or nothing will thrive.

Under the Hawthorn

Under the hawthorn
The white witch dwells
Who held in her noddle
A hundred spells,
But now she is old
As night and day,
Her memory gone
Quite far away
And try as she might
A spell to find
She can't call a single
One to mind.

She beats with her palm
The crown of her head,
She mumbles, she grumbles
From breakfast to bed,
She snaps her fingers,
She cracks her thumbs,
She whistles and whimpers,
She haws and hums,
But never a spell
Can she sing or say
Though you wait for a year,
A month and a day.

Her five wits once
Were winter-bright
As she moved on her mopstick
Through the night
In her cloak of stars,
Her pointed hat,
And safe on her shoulder
Zal the cat,
But now she sits
As cold as a stone
Her flying days
All dead and done.

Her spells that were white
As the birch-tree wood
Are vanished away
And gone for good,
And still she scrapes
Her poor old brain
But there's none will tell her
It's all in vain
As she sits under
A failing sun.

Never a body.
Never a one.

A white witch was thought to practise only 'white' or beneficial magic.

Ragged, Ragged Robin

Ragged, ragged robin
In the ditch and damp,
Light in the shade
Your red, red lamp;
Let it shine
Far and near,
Time for the cuckoo-
Call so clear.

Ragged, ragged robin
Glowing bright,
Fork-stem pointing
Left and right,
Tell the cuckoo
The month, the year;
Time the cuckoo
Was here, was here.

Ragged, ragged robin
Down by the splash,
Bring us the cuckoo
Grey as ash;
Bring us the cuckoo
Grey as slate,
Bring us the cuckoo
And bring his mate.

'Ragged robin' is a crimson flower whose real name is *Lychnis flos-cuculi*. In Greek, *luchnos* means 'lamp' and *flos-cuculi* means 'flower of the cuckoo'.

How to Protect Baby from a Witch

Bring a bap
Of salted bread
To the pillow
At his head.
Hang a wreath
Of garlic strong
By the cradle
He lies on.
(Twelve flowers
On each stem
For Christ's good men
Of Bethlehem.)
Dress the baby's
Rocking-bed
With the rowan
Green and red.
(Wicked witch
Was never seen
By the rowan's
Red and green.)

Bring the crystal
Water in,
Let the holy
Words begin,
And the priest
Or parson now
Write a cross
Upon his brow.

Changeling

No word I ever said,
Nor tear I ever shed;

My skin as fine as silk,
My breath as mild as milk.

Call me of elvish state
My glance shall prick you straight.

Left in my cot a space
Unwashed of hand and face

When once again we meet
I shall be scrubbed and sweet,

My torn and tangled hair
Be brushed and combed and fair.

Though sorrowful my eye
When mortals pass me by,

Watched as I lie alone
My sadness is quite gone,

And I shall laugh and spree
With those you may not see.

Nor beat me with a briar,
Nor burn me with the fire,

Nor leave me on the hill
In weather warm or chill,

For every hope is vain
Your own may come again,

But treat me fit and kind
That others be of mind

Your own dear child and true
Be kindly treated too.

Here, the changeling is an elf-child substituted by fairies for a mortal baby. In earlier times, an infant thought to be a changeling was often very badly treated, or left out in the open, in the hope that the fairy people would exchange it again for the baby originally stolen.

Seven Tales of Alder

1

On land, in water
I hold with sound shoot,
Stout-as-stone root,
The wasting hedge,
Bruised river banks.
Farmer, remember.
Give thanks.

2

Soft stream,
Unsleeping river,
Refound my flesh.
Men, women, ever
Use me for soles,
Use me for shoes.
No mud nor rain
Shall enter in,
Nor frost, nor hoar
Seven winters strong,
Seven summers long,
And seven more.

3

Cut my body,
Break a branch
My bright blood
You shall not stanch.
Axe me down,
I rise from ground,
Follow you over
Field and town
Ceasing only
When you leap
Over waters
Swift and deep.

4

Brush with broom
Of alder stem
From Chapman's Well
To Bethlehem
And bring me home
At Come-to-Good
In clogs of yellow
Alder wood.

5

Gather a leaf
(Round as fan)
Dew of morning
Still upon.
Every flea
In hall and home
Shall gather there
And soon be gone.

6

Hear the green song
That I sing.
I am Alder,
I am King,
Green of body,
Green of hair.
Follow me, children,
Woodman, wife,
Follow to the end
Of life;
Follow to the woods
From where
In frost or snow-shine,
Fine or rain,
Never you
Come home again.

7

Woodman, good man,
Make me a rocker
For my cradle
Said Mother Cardle.
See, it's broken and done
And my strength is gone.
Make me a rocker
For my cradle
From the alder you're chopping
For kindle.

Ask *me* first,
Said Alder.
First ask if I'm able
To spare for him
Root or limb,
Branch or bough.
Ask now,
Mother Cardle:
Or baby's bones
Won't grow
A single day
And before he's an hour
Older
His breath will fly
Far away
To a dark land
And colder.
Ask *me* first
If I'm able,
Mother Cardle,
Said Alder.

Simples and Samples

'Simples and samples,' said the White Witch.
'See what I bear in my pack.
Cures for a quinsy and cures for an itch
And one for a crick in the back.

'One for a toothache and one for a rash,
One for a burn or a scald.
One for a colic and one for a gash,
One for a head that is bald.

'One for a pimple and one for a sore,
One for a bruise or a blow.
One for sciatica, one for a snore,
One for a gathering toe.

'One for a nettle sting, one for a bee,
One for the scratch of a briar.
One for a stomach when sailing the sea,
One for St Anthony's fire.'

'White Witch,' I said as she stood in the sun,
'Have you a balm or a brew
For a true loving heart that lately was one
And now is quite broken in two?'

The white old Witch shook me her white old head
As down by my side she sat.
'Cures for a thousand, my dear,' she said.
'Never a cure for that.'

A simple is a medicine made from a single herb or plant. St Anthony's fire, also known as 'the rose' or 'the sacred fire', was a name given in earlier times to erysipelas, a fever accompanied by an acute inflammation of the skin. It was a popular belief that cures were possible through the intercession, by prayer, of St Anthony of Padua.

The Twelve O'clock Stone

Lay the child of bending bone
At midnight on the granite stone.

When the bell tells twelve o'clock
Like a cradle it shall rock.

It shall swing and it shall sway
As if it sailed upon the bay.

Straight and strong his bones shall grow
As rocks the clock-stone to and fro;

Strong as the stone that he lies on,
Though he who rocks it, none has known.

There's not a wise man in the land
Knows that arm and knows that hand:

For he who rocks the midnight stone
Is not of man and woman born.

But when the bell tells twelve o'clock
Like a cradle it shall rock

When lies a child as bare as bone
At midnight on the turning stone.

In Cornwall are a number of logan-stones: great poised boulders capable of rocking to and fro at a gentle touch. At Nancledra, in West Penwith, is such a stone: but with a difference. It was believed impossible to move it by human hand at any time, though precisely at midnight it was said to rock of its own accord like a cradle. In early times, children suffering from rickets (a disease causing a softening of the bones and resulting in such ailments as curvature of the spine and bow legs) were brought and laid on the stone in the hope of a cure.

The Apple-Tree Man

The farmer sleeps under a printed stone.
The farm it fell to the Youngest Son.
The Eldest has neither a hearth nor home.
    A sorrow and shame, said the Apple-Tree Man.

The Youngest he lends him an orchard green,
An ox and an ass and a handful of grain
And their Grannie's old cottage in Watery Lane.
    It's not what it sounds, said the Apple-Tree Man.

For the grain it was mouldy, the roof it had flown,
And never a fruit had the apple-trees grown,
The dunk was all skin and the ox was all bone.
    Here's a how-do-ye-do, said the Apple-Tree Man.

The Eldest he neither did mutter nor moan.
He found all the slates and he nailed them back on.
He laid the grass low that was lanky and long.
    Will-o'-the-Work! said the Apple-Tree Man.

He cured him his beasts with the words of a charm.
The ox and the ass to the orchard are gone,
And the apple-trees flourish as never they've done.
    Sun's coming up, said the Apple-Tree Man.

Said Youngest to Eldest, 'Now pray understand
When Quarter Day comes you must pay on demand
And dap down the rent on the palm of my hand.'
    Brotherly love! said the Apple-Tree Man.

But the Eldest had hardly the price of a pin.
Though he worked and he worried his profit was thin.
'It's wrecked and it's ruined,' he said, 'that I am!'
    Can't have that, said the Apple-Tree Man.

Two days before Christmas, all catch as catch can,
The Youngest he gives the old orchard a scan.
'Did you never hear tell of the treasure within?'
    Brother's heard of it now, said the Apple-Tree Man.

'Day after tomorrow when midnight is come
And the beasts in the shippen no longer are dumb
To task 'em and ask 'em,' he said, 'is my plan.'
    They'll tell you no lies, said the Apple-Tree Man.

'So brother,' the Youngest said, 'wake me betimes
Before Christmas comes and the church clock it chimes
And a sixpence I'll slice off your rent for a span.'
    Such bounteousness! said the Apple-Tree Man.

But the Eldest hangs holly all up in a chain
And he gives to the ox the sweet hay and good grain
And to the old donkey he gives just the same.
    Wassail! Wassail! said the Apple-Tree Man.

Then the Eldest his cider mug fills to the brim
And gives to his apple-trees out in the dim.
'I wish you Good Christmas,' he says, 'where you
    stand!'
    Look under my roots, said the Apple-Tree Man.

Says the Eldest, 'I'm blest, but it's magic that's planned
For the earth and the stones are all softer than sand.'
And a chest full of gold he digs up with his hands.
    Bide quiet and hide it, says the Apple-Tree Man.

At midnight the Eldest calls Youngest to rise
And down he comes running, the sleep in his eyes.
'Dear ox and dear donkey, please tell if you can
Where lies the gold treasure that's under my land?'

The gold and the treasure are taken and gone
And you never shall find it by moon or by sun
Though all the wide world you may search and may scan,
     Said the ox and the ass and the Apple-Tree Man.

The source of this story is a legend from Somerset documented in *Folk Tales of England* edited by Katharine M. Briggs and Ruth L. Tongue (Routledge, 1965) and also in Katharine Briggs's *A Dictionary of Fairies* (Allen Lane, 1976). The Apple-Tree Man was the name given to the oldest apple-tree in an orchard, and in which the fertility of the entire orchard was thought to dwell.

   According to an ancient custom in this part of Britain, it was the youngest and not the eldest son who inherited a property on the death of the parent. By virtue of his age, the eldest son was assumed to have had time to make his way, and make good in the world. In the story here, the eldest was regarded with favour by the Apple-Tree Man because he saw to the restoration of the health and fertility of the ruined orchard, and also because he wassailed the trees by pouring draughts of cider over them: a custom still followed in certain districts of Somerset.

On the Eve of St Thomas

On the Eve of St Thomas
I walked the grey wood
Though mammy she told me
That I never should,

And there did I meet
(Though never one spoke)
Kit-with-the-Canstick,[1]
The Man in the Oak,

Tom Tumbler and Boneless
And Whistle-the-Fife,
Derrick and Puddlefoot,
Gooseberry Wife,

[1] candlestick

Changeling, Hob Goblin,
Bull-Beggar and Hag,
Tom Thumb and Puckle,
Long-Jack-with-the-Bag.

They nidded and nodded
And winked me an eye,
They bent and they bowed to me
As I passed by.

Was never a shudder
Nor ever a scream,
The wood was as silent
As it were a dream.

Though still were their voices
Their lips told me clear
They wished me Good Christmas
And many a year.

They never did blatter
Nor shiver nor shriek,
Nor clamour nor yammer
Nor rustle nor screak

As they pointed my path
By bramble and brake,
Waved each a pale hand
As my leave I did take.

And I thought I could tell
As I said them goodbye
Though their lips they did smile
That sad was each eye

As out the grey wood
I went on my way
To hearth and to home
And St Thomas's Day.

In ancient times it was believed that goblins and ghosts of all kinds were
likely to be seen particularly between St Thomas's Eve (20 December) and
Christmas Eve.

I am the Song

I am the song that sings the bird.
I am the leaf that grows the land.
I am the tide that moves the moon.
I am the stream that halts the sand.
I am the cloud that drives the storm.
I am the earth that lights the sun.
I am the fire that strikes the stone.
I am the clay that shapes the hand.
I am the word that speaks the man.

Odds and Ends

'Quack!' Said the Billy-goat

'Quack!' said the billy-goat.
  'Oink!' said the hen.
'Miaow!' said the little chick
  Running in the pen.

'Hobble-gobble!' said the dog.
  'Cluck!' said the sow.
'Tu-whit tu-whoo!' the donkey said.
  'Baa!' said the cow.

'Hee-haw!' the turkey cried.
  The duck began to moo.
All at once the sheep went,
  'Cock-a-doodle-doo!'

The owl coughed and cleared his throat
  And he began to bleat.
'Bow-wow!' said the cock
  Swimming in the leat.

'Cheep-cheep!' said the cat
  As she began to fly.
'Farmer's been and laid an egg –
  That's the reason why.'

Charity Chadder

Charity Chadder
Borrowed a ladder,
Leaned it against the moon,
Climbed to the top
Without a stop
On the 31st of June,
Brought down every single star,
Kept them all in a pickle jar.

Dear Me

Dear me, but haven't you heard?
Barnaby Robbins turned into a bird.
His back is brown, his nose is a beak
And there's much more colour come into his cheek.

He's part of him white, and instead of a vest
He's a lot of red feathers all over his chest.
He hasn't a tooth in the whole of his head
And as for toes, he's claws instead.

He bobs his noddle and flirts his tail
As he hops and stops on the orchard rail,
And here's a thing that made me squirm:
I saw him eating a garden worm.

I asked young Barnaby what was wrong
But all he did was sing me a song.
'Barney,' I said, 'don't take it amiss –
But you simply can't go on behaving like this.'

'Barney,' I said, 'will you listen to me?'
But he flew to the top of the sycamore tree.
'Barney,' I said, 'you'll be sorry one day.'
But he whistled a tune and he flew away.

I Took My Wife to Market

I took my wife to market,
   It was not market day.
We had a hundred hens' eggs
   That never a fowl did lay.

We rode there in a trap, sir,
   Had neither wheel nor brake,
And from the yellow stable
   The pony did not take.

When we got to the market
   It was the crack of noon,
High in the tower the hooting owl
   And in the sky the moon.

And when we sold the eggs, sir,
   For neither coin nor gear,
We went into an ale-house
   That sold not wine nor beer.

We sat down by the churchyard
   When to eat we were fain.
The cheese it was not made of milk,
   Nor the bread from grain.

And when the fair was over
   We made our homeward way,
Deep in the west the dying moon
   And in the east the day.

I opened up my door, sir,
    No latch nor key had I,
And as we went downstairs to bed
    I heard the cockerel cry.

Although for years a thousand
    Upon this earth I be,
I want not such a day again
    For all the Queen's fee.

And though for years a thousand
    On earth I may grow old
I want not such a day again
    For all the King's gold.

I Don't Want to Grumble

'I don't want to grumble,' said Sally the Mouse.
'I don't want to grumble at all,
And I don't want to grouse, but they've brought home
   a HOUSE
And it hangs on the living-room wall.

'It's painted and polished as clean as a pin,
But here's something that gave me a shock:
From somewhere within there's a sound that's akin
To a curious tick and a tock.

'And the worst of the matter (of this there's no doubt)
Is each day and each night, through and through,
There's a terrible shout from a bird that flies out
And calls everybody cuckoo!

'Such conduct,' said Sally, 'is simply absurd
As I frequently try to explain,
But that ill-mannered bird just ignores every word
And flies forwards *and backwards* again.

'My children can't sleep and their heads they are sore
And our dear little homestead they shun.
I'm not at all sure I can stand any more.
Will you please tell me what's to be done?'

As I Went Down Zig Zag

As I went down Zig Zag
   The clock striking one,
I saw a man cooking
   An egg in the sun.

           As I went down Zig Zag
              The clock striking two,
           I watched a man walk
              With one boot and one shoe.

As I went down Zig Zag
   The clock striking three,
I heard a man murmuring
   'Buzz!' like a bee.

           As I went down Zig Zag
              The clock striking four,
           I saw a man swim
              In no sea by no shore.

As I went down Zig Zag
   The clock striking five,
I caught a man keeping
   A hog in a hive.

As I went down Zig Zag
  The clock striking six,
I met a man making
  A blanket of bricks.

As I went down Zig Zag
  The clock striking seven,
A man asked me if
  I was odd or was even.

As I went down Zig Zag
  The clock striking eight,
I saw a man sailing
  A seven-barred gate.

As I went down Zig Zag
  The clock striking nine,
I saw a man milking
  Where never were kine.

As I went down Zig Zag
　　The clock striking ten,
I watched a man waltz
　　With a cock and a hen.

As I went down Zig Zag
　　The clock striking eleven,
I saw a man baking
　　A loaf with no leaven.

As I went down Zig Zag
　　The clock striking twelve,
For dyes from the rainbow
　　I saw a man delve.

So if you'd keep your senses,
　　The point of my rhyme
Is don't go down Zig Zag
　　When the clocks start to chime.

Zig Zag is the name of a steep footpath in Launceston.

The Song of the Shapes

Miss Triangle, Miss Rectangle,
　　Miss Circle and Miss Square
Went walking down on Shipshape Shore
　　To taste the sea-salt air.
They talked of this, they talked of that,
　　From a, b, c, to z.
But most of all they talked about
　　The day they would be wed.

'My sweetheart is a sailor blue!'
　　Miss Circle sang with joy,
'And dreams of me when out at sea
　　Or swinging round the buoy;
When homeward bound for Plymouth Sound
　　Or sailing by the Nore,
Or gazing through the port-hole
　　At some shining foreign shore.

'And when we both are married,
　　Up at the Villa Sphere
We'll have a Christmas pudding
　　Each evening of the year;
And ring-a-ring o'-roses
　　We'll dance at night and noon,
Whether the sun is shining
　　Or if it is the moon.'

'Good gracious!' cried Miss Triangle,
   'But it's quite plain to see
What might be best for you and yours
   Won't do for mine and me.
He plays the balalaika
   In a Russian Gypsy Band
All up and down the country
   And in many a foreign land.

'He loves the dusty desert,
   The camels and the sun,
And sits and thinks beside the Sphinx
   Of when we shall be one.
He's bought for us a dream-house
   By shady palm-trees hid.
Do say you all will pay a call
   At Little Pyramid.'

'My boy so rare,' then said Miss Square,
  'Is different yet again.
His world is one of timber,
  Of chisel and of plane.
I might have wed a constable,
  I might have wed a vet,
But fairly on a carpenter
  My heart is squarely set.

'Our own dear home won't be a cone,
  A cylinder (or tube),
But just a quiet cottage
  At the village of All Cube.
And you must come and visit us
  Each Saturday at three
For sticky buns and cake (with plums)
  And sugar-lumps and tea.'

'Though pleasant,' sighed Miss Rectangle,
    'To walk among these rocks is,
I'd sooner far be where my dar-
    ling's making cardboard boxes.
He makes them big, he makes them small,
    He makes them short and long,
And all the day (his workmates say)
    He sings a sort of song.

'My bride and I one day will fly
    Beside the Spanish sea
And live in Casa Cuboid
    Which we've built above the quay.
It has a special corner
    For fishing with a line
And catching of fish-fingers
    For friends who come to dine.'

Miss Triangle, Miss Rectangle,
    Miss Circle and Miss Square
Came walking up from Shipshape Shore
    Without a single care.
But pray remember if you play
    The match and marriage game
Opposites often suit as well
    As those who seem the same.

As I Went Down the Cat-walk

As I went down the cat-walk
   Where all the catkins blow,
I saw an old cat-burglar
   Beside a cattalo.[1]
And O he miaowed and O he mewed
   Just like the cat-bird's call.
I said, 'Pray cease this catalogue
   Of scatty caterwaul.
I didn't catch your name, I fear,
   But how, my dear old chap,
Among such cataracts of tears
   May I take my cat-nap?'

[1] cross between a buffalo and a cow

He said, 'Of various cat-calls
   I'm running the gamut
Because upon my cat-fish
   No catsup has been put!
Such catchpenny behaviour
   It makes me ill, then iller.'
I said, 'Please don't excite yourself.
   Lean on this caterpillar.'
I plucked from off the apple tree
   A juicy, ripe cat's-head.
He took it with some cat-lap
   And felt much better fed.
And then he played cat's-cradle
   And turned cat in the pan,
And sailed to Catalonia
   All in a catamaran.
He sailed away by Catalan Bay[2]
   That happy cataman.

[2] in Gibraltar

Old Mrs Thing-um-e-bob

Old Mrs Thing-um-e-bob
  Lives at you-know-where,
Dropped her what-you-may-call-it down
  The well of the kitchen stair.

'Gracious me!' said Thing-um-e-bob,
  'This don't look too bright.
I'll ask old Mr What's-his-name
  To try and put it right.'

Along came Mr What's-his-name,
  He said, 'You've broke the lot!
I'll have to see what I can do
  With some of the you-know-what.'

So he gave the what-you-may-call-it a pit
  And he gave it a bit of a pat,
And he put it all together again
  With a little of this and that.

And he gave the what-you-may-call-it a dib
  And he gave it a dab as well
When all of a sudden he heard a note
  As clear as any bell.

'It's as good as new!' cried What's-his-name.
  'But please remember, now,
In future Mrs Thing-um-e-bob
  You'll have to go you-know-how.'

There Was a Young Snowman

There was a young snowman of Churton-le-Grice[1]
Who made up his mind he would stay in one piece,
And whether the weather was hot or was cool
He'd never turn into a puddle or pool.

Each winter-white night when the temperature fell
He took off his scarf and his topper as well,
He took off his jacket, and all on his own
He froze himself solid as iron or stone.

In springtime the swallows around him all flew.
In summer he smiled in the green and the blue.
In autumn he watched the leaves skim down the lane,
And in winter he froze up all over again.

But soon the good people of Churton-le-Grice
Grew weary of hearing (and quite without cease),
'It's a cold-hearted folk who live here, I'll be bound,
Where even a snowman lasts all the year round!'

So the Churtoners built them a battering ram.
They lit a big bonfire. They all shouted, 'Scram!'
They pushed with a tractor, they pulled with a trawl,
But they just couldn't shift the young snowman at all.

[1] pronounced 'Greece'

'It's simple,' they said, 'and quite perfectly plain
That this singular snowman would rather remain.
We must pay no regard to what others may say.
If he likes us *that* much, why not ask him to stay?'

And if on your travels, for any good reason,
You happen by Churton (whatever the season)
Remember the snowman who stood on the hill
In yesterday's weather. You'll find him there still.

One for the Man

One for the man who lived by the sand,
Two for his son and daughter,
Three for the sea-birds washed so white
That flew across the water.

Four for the sails that brought the ship
About the headland turning.
Five for the jollyboys in her shrouds,
Six for the sea-lamps burning.

Seven for the sacks of silver and gold
They sailed through the winter weather.
Eight for the places set on shore
When they sat down together.

Nine for the songs they sang night-long,
Ten for the candles shining.
Eleven for the lawmen on the hill
As they all were sweetly dining.

Twelve for the hour that struck as they stood
To the Judge so careful and clever.
Twelve for the years that must come and go
And we shall see them never.

Green Man, Blue Man

As I was walking through Guildhall Square
I smiled to see a green man there,
But when I saw him coming near
My heart was filled with nameless fear.

As I was walking through Madford Lane
A blue man stood there in the rain.
I asked him in by my front-door,
For I'd seen a blue man before.

As I was walking through Landlake Wood
A grey man in the forest stood,
But when he turned and said, 'Good day'
I shook my head and ran away.

As I was walking by Church Stile
A purple man spoke there a while.
I spoke to him because, you see,
A purple man once lived by me.

But when the night falls dark and fell
How, O how, am I to tell,
Grey man, green man, purple, blue,
Which is which is which of you?

Jack

Jack-o'-the-Bowl[1] drinks the cream in the byre
Jack-in-the-Smoke turns the spit by the fire

Jack-in-the-Pulpit[2] grows in the deep wood
Jack-in-the-Irons[3] is up to no good

Jack-in-the-Box jumps about on a spring
Jack-o'-the-Clock makes the hour bell ring

Jack-in-the-Basket[4] stands in the sea-spray
Jack-o'-the-Lantern will lead you astray

Jack-in-the-Green wears the leaves of a tree
Jack-in-the-Cellar's a baby to be

Jack-in-a-Bottle[5] fine feathers a nest
Jack-out-of-Office is taking a rest

Jack-at-a-Pinch gives a hand when he can
Jack-by-the-Hedge[6] stands up straight as a man

Jack-a-Dreams dozes all day in the sun
Jack-of-all-Trades is . . .

[1] house ghost or goblin
[2] North American wild plant
[3] tall ghostly figure, frightens the traveller
[4] basket on a pole, indicating a sandbank
[5] long-tailed titmouse, builds a bottle-shaped nest
[6] plant of the wallflower family, sometimes called garlic mustard

Songs and Stories

Baby, Baby

Baby, baby
In the walking water,
Are you my sister's
Darling daughter?

My sister, they said,
Who went to Spain
And vowed she'd never
Come home again?

Her eyes were the self-same
Periwinkle-blue
And she wore a locket
Just like you.

She wore a shawl
Of Honiton lace
Like the one that drifts
About your face.

Baby, don't stray
Where the tall weeds swim.
Fetch the boat, Billy,
And bring the baby in.

My Name is Little Mosie

My name is Little Mosie,
I lie among the bushes,
My cradle is a sailing-boat
Of yellow reeds and rushes.

It was my sister brought me
Beside the swimming water.
One morning very early came
The King of Egypt's daughter.

She took me to her palace,
She laid me in her bed,
She dressed me in the finest shirt
Of gold and silver thread.

She put a circlet on my brow,
A ring upon my hand,
'And you shall be,' she said to me,
'A Prince of Egypt land.'

But now, in a far country,
I tend my field-flock well
And none there is to listen
To the mystery I tell:

When I was Little Mosie
I lay among the bushes
Cradled in a sailing-boat
Of yellow reeds and rushes.

Lady Jane Grey

Lady Jane Grey
    Went on her way
Out of her house
    On the first of May.

The blackbird whistled,
    The blackbird sang
And all the bells
    Of England rang.

She went to the palace.
    She sat her down.
She wore the Queen
    Of England's crown.

She wore it a week
    And a day and a day
Of her sixteen years.
    Poor Lady Jane Grey.

Riverside

When you were born at Riverside,
My mother said to me,
It rained for nights, it rained for days
And then some more, said she.

And all at once came riding
The water with a roar
Along the river valley
Down from Bodmin Moor.

The water came in at the window,
It came in at the door,
It swallowed up the cellar,
It came up through the floor.

It filled up every kettle,
It filled up every crock,
It swam around the fireplace,
It filled the long-case clock.

It climbed the kitchen dresser,
It climbed the kitchen chairs,
It climbed up on the table,
It climbed the kitchen stairs.

And as we wailed and wondered
If we should sink or float,
My father came to Riverside
In a sailing-boat.

He took me and my mother
To move upon the swell,
My brother Shem, my brother Ham,
Their families as well.

He took him food and fodder
To sail upon the blue,
He took aboard all creatures
By two and two and two.

And after days and after nights
Watching the waters pour,
We landed on a mountain-top
Somewhere by Wise Man's Tor.

All this, my mother told me,
Was when I was in my pram,
And next door lived my brother Shem,
And next to him lived Ham.

This tale my mother told me
The truth that I might say
Of when I lived at Riverside
Yesterday.

When I Went up to Avignon

When I went up to Avignon
With Jean le Bon the butcher's son,
In from the country, and as green,
We signed for seven at seventeen.
Dressed in red and dressed in blue
We walked and talked as the soldiers do.
     Tan-tan-tan!
     Fol-di-ro!

They gave us the gun, they gave us the blade,
They told us the tricks of the soldier's trade.
In rain and snow, in hail and sun,
Our paths were two that had been one,
And many a blow we gave, we bore,
For heavy is the hand of war.
     Tan-tan-tan!
     Fol-di-ro!

When seven long years were lost and won
We came again to Avignon
And I said to Jean of the butcher's knife,
'What shall you do for the rest of life?'
And Jean he smiled and I heard him say,
'My butcher's gear I'll throw away!'

> *Tan-tan-tan!*
> *Fol-di-ro!*

'My sharpening steel I'll put in store
And I'll ply the butcher's skill no more.
I'll lay on the fire my butcher's clothes.
I'll grow me a peach, I'll grow me a rose.
I'll grow me the grape till the day I die.
Never ask the reason why.'

> *Tan-tan-tan!*
> *Fol-di-ro!*

Lord Lovelace

Lord Lovelace rode home from the wars,
His wounds were black as ice,
While overhead the winter sun
Hung out its pale device.

The lance was tattered in his hand,
Sundered his axe and blade,
And in a bloody coat of war
Lord Lovelace was arrayed.

And he was sick and he was sore
But never sad was he,
And whistled bright as any bird
Upon an April tree.

'Soon, soon,' he cried, 'at Lovelace Hall
Fair Ellen I shall greet,
And she with loving heart and hand
Will make my sharp wounds sweet.

'And Young Jehan the serving-man
Will bring the wine and bread,
And with a yellow link will light
Us to the bridal bed.'

But when he got to Lovelace Hall
Burned were both wall and stack,
And in the stinking moat the tower
Had tumbled on its back.

And none welcomed Lord Lovelace home
Within the castle shell,
And ravaged was the land about
That Lord Lovelace knew well.

Long in his stirrups Lovelace stood
Before his broken door,
And slowly rode he down the hill
Back to the bitter war.

Nor mercy showed he from that day,
Nor tear fell from his eye,
And rich and poor both fearful were
When Black Lovelace rode by.

This tale is true that now I tell
To woman and to man,
As Fair Ellen is my wife's name
And mine is Young Jehan.

The Obby Oss

Early one morning,
    Second of May,
Up jumped the Obby Oss,
    Said, 'I'm away!'

With his tall dunce-head
    And his canvas gown
He tiptoed the streets
    Of Padstow town.

The wild, wild ponies
    Of Bodmin Moor
Said, 'Go back, Obby,
    To Padstow shore!

'With your snappers of oak
    And your tail of horse
You can't come running
    On this race-course.'

He went to Helston,
    He jigged, he danced,
And in and out
    Of the houses pranced.

'You can't stop here,'
    They said, said they,
'If you won't dance the furry
    In the Helston way.'

He went to Brown Willy
   On the Eve of St John.
They said, 'Who's that
   With the black kilt on?

'You'll soon run, Obby,
   To your drinking-trough
When the midsummer fire
   Burns your top-knot off!'

He went to St Ives
   Where on the height
Danced ten pretty maids
   All dressed in white.

And round they ran
   To the fiddler's moan
In the waking light
   By John Knill's stone.

He went to St Columb
   For the hurling game.
'You must go back, Obby,
   From where you came!

'For high in the air
   Flies the silver ball,
And Obby can't catch
   Or kick at all.'

The County Council
  Gave a county stare,
Said, 'Who's that dancing
  With his legs all bare?

'Go back, Obby,
  To Padstow Bar
As quick as the light
  Of a shooting star.'

The people of Padstow
  Night and day
Watched for Obby
  Like the first of May.

Without old Obby
  And his dancing drum
They feared that the summer
  Never would come.

When April ended
  At the bell's first beat,
Obby came dancing
  Down the street.

'Welcome, Obby!'
  He heard them cheer,
'For we love you the best
  Of the Padstow year.'

'Never again
   Will I run or roam,'
Said Obby, 'from Padstow
   My own true home.

'See the sun is rising,
   It dries up the dew,
That we may welcome summer
   As we belong to do.'

The Obby Oss is a primitive figure carried by a dancer round the port of Padstow, on the north coast of Cornwall, every year on 1 May to herald the arrival of summer. It is accompanied by music, dancing and a great deal of merry-making. All the other festivals mentioned are still held in Cornwall: for instance, a chain of bonfires is lit throughout the county on Midsummer Eve, the Eve of St John, since Midsummer Day is also the feast of St John the Baptist.

When the Cornish say that they 'belong to' do something, they mean that it is right and proper for something to be done: that it is a personal responsibility.

Let Us Walk to the Williwaw Islands

'Let us walk to the Williwaw Islands,'
Said the porcupine-pig to the snoar.
'If we turn to the right by the Isle of Wight
We'll be there by a quarter to four.'

'Never once have I gazed on the ocean,'
Said the snoar to the porcupine-pig.
'How I wish I could stray through its waters one day!
But isn't it awfully *big*?

'And I've heard that the waves of the briny
Are inclined to be salty and steep
Should one venture out more than ten yards from the
    shore –
And isn't it frightfully deep?'

'I can't think,' then replied his companion,
'Where you get such ideas, and that's flat.
A very old spoof who once sat on the roof
Told me something quite different from that.

'He remarked that the bright-bluey water
Stood quite still in the stiffest of breeze,
And the sea-salty waste had a sugary taste
And barely came up to one's knees.

'And he said that the Williwaw Islands
Are constructed of coconut cream
And Belgian chocs and peppermint rocks
And orange-and-lemonade streams.

'I foresee both our lives very shortly
Becoming a terrible bore.
Time to get off the shelf! Find things out for oneself!'
Said the porcupine-pig to the snoar.

'On reflection, my dearest old crony,
I can do nothing more than agree.
Let us hurry away without further delay,'
Said the snoar to the porcupine-p.

So they packed up their goods and their chattels
(Whatever a chattel may be),
Some biscuits and bread and a buttery spread
And they hurried away to the sea.

But when, at the edge of the ocean,
They gazed at its foam and its fret,
Said the snoar, 'Gracious me, my friend porcupine-p.,
It's the frightfullest thing I've seen yet!'

For the water it tumbled and twisted
And jumped up right out of the bay,
And it just wasn't true that its colour was blue
But a horrible sort of a grey.

It wouldn't stand still for a moment.
It did nothing but surge and then swell.
It held a big ship in its watery grip
And it broke pieces off it as well.

Said the porcupine-pig, 'I've a feeling
As I gaze at the sea and the skies
That to walk all those miles to the Williwaw Isles
Might turn out to be rather unwise.'

And the snoar, who was sensibly smiling,
He lifted a sensible thumb,
And they turned in their track and they made their
   way back
The very same way they had come.

'We don't care for candy,' they chanted.
'Nor for sweets nor for treats large or small,
But if there's a spoof resting up on your roof
We'd be glad if you gave us a call, that's all.
We'd be glad if you gave us a call.'

What Happened

What happened to Jonathan Still,
Cider-sour, all smothered in flour,
Used to work Ridgegrove Mill?
    Off on a long stay
    With gran and grand, they say,
    Under the hill.

Never seem to see Tom Black –
Marched with the men, nineteen-I-don't-know-when,
With rifle and pack.
    Showed his soldier face
    In some foreign space.
    Never came back.

Where's Sulky Dick Sloppy, so small, so slim,
Used to mooch by with rod, basket and fly
To doze on the river brim?
    Trying the water
    This year and a quarter,
    Taking a deep swim.

Do you know where is Tamasine Long,
Her with the green stare, the guinea-gold hair?
Went wandering with Singing Ben Strong?
    Never returned –
    Maybe she learned
    A different song.

What happened to Fidgety Goodge, Tinker John,
Little Tim Spy, him with the bad eye,
Beulah and Billy Fireworks, kept *The Swan*?
  Couldn't keep track of 'em,
  Never one of the pack of 'em.
  All gone, gone.

Leonardo

Leonardo, painter, taking
   Morning air
     On Market Street
Saw the wild birds in their cages
   Silent in
     The dust, the heat.

Took his purse from out his pocket
   Never questioning
     The fee,
Bore the cages to the green shade
   Of a hill-top
     Cypress tree.

'What you lost,' said Leonardo,
   'I now give to you
     Again,
Free as noon and night and morning,
   As the sunshine,
     As the rain.'

And he took them from their prisons,
   Held them to
      The air, the sky;
Pointed them to the bright heaven.
   'Fly!' said Leonardo.
      'Fly!'

This story is told of the Italian painter Leonardo da Vinci (1452–1519).

There Was an Old Woman

There was an old woman of Whittingham Firth
Who hadn't a friend on the face of the earth,
Or so all the people who lived thereabout
Were perfectly certain and hadn't a doubt.

'To get to her cottage,' they all would explain,
'You must walk to the end of Deepwatery Lane,
'You must cross seven meadows and climb seven stiles
And there isn't a neighbour for miles and miles.'

The folk in the village said, 'Isn't it sad?
That silly old thing must be really quite mad!
A body must be in a terrible plight
With no-one to talk to from morning till night.

'Though we're none of us gossips, we vow and declare
There's tittle and tattle we all like to share.
It must be like living your life in a doze
With never a notion of how the world goes.'

But the little old woman who lived in the cot
Hadn't time to be lonely or time to be not,
For what with one thing and another, it's true,
She'd never a minute with nothing to do.

Each morning the moment that day had begun
She rose from her pillow as sharp as the sun,
And if skies they were shining or skies they were dour
She'd put on the kettle at just the same hour.

When breakfast was done, and the dishes done too,
She'd sweep and she'd polish her little house through.
She baked and she cooked, and as sweet as a dream
She worked her green garden that lay by the stream.

The robin and blackbird they came at her call
And so did the hedgehog lived under the wall,
And every creature came passing that way
She gave them a smile and she spoke them good-day.

And good-night to the moon every evening she said
As, her cat coming after, she went to her bed:
That lonely old woman of Whittingham Firth
Who hadn't a friend on the face of the earth.

1, 2, 3, 4

1, 2, 3, 4,
Over the mountain,
Over the moor,
Here comes the soldier
Home from war.
    Tan-tan-tan!

4, 3, 2, 1,
Foul or fine,
Snow or sun,
Take it from me
It wasn't fun.

After the battle the Sergeant said,
'You've legs and arms
And you kept your head
And you're stony broke
But you're not stone dead.'

No more marching, no more drill,
I'm on my way
Down Homeward Hill
And I thank my stars
I'm breathing still.

'Take your pack, be on your way,'
I heard the Sergeant-
Major say,
'And live to fight
Another day.'
    Tan-tan-tan!

Times and Places

Early in the Morning

Early in the morning
The water hits the rocks,
The birds are making noises
Like old alarum clocks,
The soldier on the skyline
Fires a golden gun
And over the back of the chimney-stack
Explodes the silent sun.

Twenty-four Hours

Twenty-four hours
   Make a night and a day;
Never a minute
   More will one stay.

One o'clock sounds
   To the owl's cold cry;
Two, as the flame of the fox
   Glimmers by.

Three, the still hour
   Of the moon and the star;
Four, the first cock-crow
   Is heard from afar.

Five, and the bird-song
   Already begun;
Six, the bright mail van
   Comes up with the sun.

Seven, here's the milk
   With the butter and cream;
Eight, all the kettles
   Are letting off steam.

Nine, the school bell
   Calls the lazy and late;
Ten, as the children
   Chant, 'Two fours are eight.'

Eleven, and it's cooking
    With pot, pan and spoon;
Twelve, and the morning
    Says, 'Good afternoon!'

One, and for dinner
    Hot pudding and pie;
Two, all the dishes
    Are watered and dry.

Three, the quick water-hen
    Hides in the pool;
Four, as the children
    Come smiling from school.

Five, see the milking cows
    Lurch down the lane;
Six, and the family
    Together again.

Seven, and the children
    Are bathed and in bed;
Eight, dad is snoozing,
    The paper unread.

Nine, and the house mouse
   Squints out of his hole;
Ten, and the tabby cat
   Takes a dark stroll.

Eleven, bolt the window
   And lock the front door;
Twelve o'clock strikes
   And on sea and on shore
Night and day's journey
   Is starting once more.
Twelve o'clock sounds
   On the steep and the plain,
Day and night's journey
   Beginning again.

All Day Saturday

Let it sleet on Sunday,
Monday let it snow,
Let the mist on Tuesday
From the salt-sea flow.
Let it hail on Wednesday,
Thursday let it rain,
Let the wind on Friday
Blow a hurricane,
But Saturday, Saturday
Break fair and fine
And all day Saturday
Let the sun shine.

I Want to be Monday

'I want to be Monday,' said Friday.
'It's such a dull spot that I've got.
I'd much rather have it than my day
That comes almost last of the lot.'

'What nonsense!' said Tuesday to Thursday.
'I don't think she knows what she's at.
There's no telling which is the worst day
Or which is the best, come to that.'

And Wednesday whispered to Sunday,
'I hope Monday doesn't say yes.
I've a feeling by changing the one day
We'll get in a terrible mess.'

Said Monday to Friday, 'A poor day?
But there's no one of whom we could speak
Who don't thank the stars that it's your day
At the end of a workaday week.'

'Of all the seven days,' declared Friday,
'I never thought I was the star!
If it's really that happy and high a day
I think I'll leave things as they are.
Yes, I think I'll leave things as they are.'

Tuesday Monday

Tuesday Monday
On a Sunday
Went to Saturday
For the one day;
Lost her way
At Hot Cross Friday
Found it again
By Thursday Highway.
Drove her car
But couldn't park it
Till she came
To Wednesday Market.
How to get home
After her fun day?
'Back to front,'
Said Tuesday Monday.

Round the Town

Round the town with Billy,
  Round the town with Sue,
  From Sunday morning to Saturday night
  With nothing else to do.

What do you do on Monday?
  We look up at the sky
  Waiting for a drying wind
  To make the washing fly.

What do you do on Tuesday?
  From underneath the stair
  We see them take the wooden horse
  To let the linen air.

What do you do on Wednesday?
  We watch the butchers' men
  Drive the frightened animals
  In and out the pen.

What do you do on Thursday?
  On early-closing day
  We see the shops are safely locked
  And the money put away.

What do you do on Friday?
  The local paper's read
  To find if we are still alive
  Or whether we are dead.

What do you do on Saturday?
  We sit and hold our breath
  And see the silver cowboys
  Shoot themselves to death.

What do you do on Sunday?
  We listen for the bell
  And pray to Christ our Saviour
  To guard and keep us well.

What do you do on Monday?
  We look out through the pane
  And if it's wet or if it's fine
  Begin all over again.

Quarter-jacks

Tom and Tim the quarter-boys
On the Guildhall Tower
Turn and strike the quarter-bell
Twenty times an hour.
Over the swimming river
They stare as straight as light
Except when Tom turns to the left
And Tim turns to the right.
They stand as stiff as iron
Above the moving bay
Waiting for the quarter
And to beat the time away.
Their bonnets are black, are scarlet,
Their suits are yellow, are blue,
Their collars and cuffs are silver
As the buckle on each shoe,
And on the Guildhall Tower
In weather foul or clear
They stand as smart as Sunday
All through the year.

Whether the sun is shining
Or if the moon is high
They stand their ground above the town
Under a Cornish sky.
The day that I first saw them
Is a day long sped,
And never a word I spoke, for there
Was nothing to be said.
The day that I first saw them
Is a day long done
And those who stood beside me
Silent are and gone.
Tom and Tim the quarter-boys
On the Guildhall Tower
Still they strike the quarter-bell
Twenty times an hour:
Tom and Tim the quarter-boys
Standing side by side
Over the changing water,
The turning of the tide.

Jackie Grimble

Here's Jackie Grimble
Looking in the window
Pointing at the mountain
Pointing at the moor.
Shall we walk together
In the golden weather?
Calls Jackie Grimble.
That's what it's for!

Here's Jackie Grimble
With his arms akimbo
Winks a wicked eye at me
As if to say,
Never mind your master,
The clock is beating faster,
The sun will be a cinder
Before the end of day.

Here's Jackie Grimble
Thinner than a spindle
Pointing where the emerald
Grasses grow.
Why must you labour
With pencil and with paper,
Says Jackie Grimble,
When the sun shines so?

Ah, but Jackie Grimble
The air is growing nimble,
A white wind is rising
That smells of snow.
Under the green riding
The tall mire is hiding
And the sands are quick
Wherever I go.

Here's Jackie Grimble
No bigger than a thimble
Dancing, advancing
Down from the tor.
Lie in the clover
Before the summer's over,
Cries Jackie Grimble,
That's what it's for!

Summer Was Always Sun

Summer was always sun,
Winter was made of snow,
Forward the spring, the fall
Was slow.

Down from the moor the stream
Ran swift, ran clear.
The trees were leaved with song
For all to hear.

The seas, the skies were blue.
With stars the beach was sown.
Printing the endless shore,
A child: barefoot, alone.

What is this time, this place?
I hear you say.
When was the wide world so?
Yesterday.

I Went to Santa Barbara

I went to Santa Barbara,
I saw upon the pier
Four-and-twenty lobster pots
And a barrel of German beer.

The ships in the bay sailed upside-down,
The trees went out with the tide,
The river escaped from the ocean
And over the mountainside.

High on the hill the Mission
Broke in two in the sun.
The bell fell out of the turning tower
And struck the hour of one.

I heard a hundred fishes fly
Singing across the lake
When I was in Santa Barbara
And the earth began to shake.

My friend Gregor Antonio,
Was with me all that day,
Says it is all inside my head
And there's nothing in what I say.

But I was in Santa Barbara
And in light as bright as snow
I see it as if it were yesterday
Or a hundred years ago.

Venton Ham

Said Jack to Jim
And Jim to Sam,
'Remember how
The water swam
Over the weir
At Venton Ham?
There we walked,
There we ran,
There we fished
Above the dam.
There we wandered
Up and down
Under the grey eye
Of the town.'

Said Jim to Sam
And Sam to Jack,
'In all these years
I've not been back.'
'Nor I,' said Jack,
'And I declare
We ought to see
How things are there,
For days and months
They hurry on
And come next week
We might be gone.'

So Jim and Jack
And also Sam
Hobbled the path
To Venton Ham:
Two with whiskers,
One with a peg
And each as bald
As an ostrich egg.
And all the way
Each mother's son
Nattered and chattered
Of days long done;
Walked and talked
The hour away
Till there was nothing
More to say.

And Jack and Sam
And also Jim
They sat them by
The river rim.
They sat them where
The water sped
And neither spoke
Nor either said,
And all the day
They sat them there
They thought of times
That vanished were:
And first of spring,
Of autumn come,
Blackthorn winter,
Summer sun.

There was no need
To say a word
As each perched easy
As a bird
And watched where
The sweet water sang
Over the weir
At Venton Ham;
Over the weir
Falling free
Down the long valley
To the sea.

Let's Go Ride

Let's go ride in a sleigh, Johanna,
Let's go ride in a sleigh,
Through the mountains,
Under the trees,
Over the ice
On Lake Louise.
Let's go ride in a sleigh, Johanna,
    – There's only five dollars to pay.

Let's go ride today, Johanna,
Let's go ride today,
The horses shaking
Their silver traces,
The branches flaking
Snow on our faces.
Let's go ride today, Johanna,
    – There's only five dollars to pay.

Let's go ride while we may, Johanna,
Let's go ride while we may,
By the tall ice-fall
And the frozen spring
As the frail sun shines
And the sleigh-bells ring.
Let's go ride while we may, Johanna,
      – There's only five dollars to pay.

Bramblepark

Bramblepark Cottage,
Bramblepark Well,
Sleep in the sound
Of St Stephen's bell.

Only the chimney-stack
Stands up high.
The cottage is burst
And roofed with sky.

The bright grass litters
Bramblepark Lane.
The wash-house tub
Is filled with rain.

Here's a rusted saw;
A broken crock.
A bath with no bottom
Brims nettle and dock.

The one-tree bridge
Is fallen and gone
Where the easy trout
Hid under a stone.

Here we blackberried,
Here we swam,
Made out of pebbles and mud
A dam.

Here the tall heron
Fished the stream.
Here we watched
The kingfisher gleam.

Down the long valley
The wood-pigeons cry
Where the Padstow to Waterloo
Train steamed by.

But when the day
Slides into the dark
Over the valley
At Bramblepark,

Whose is the voice
I know so well
Sounding within
The cottage shell?

And whose is the hand
That strikes a spark
For the evening lamp
At Bramblepark?

Is it the light
Of moon or star,
The little bold owl
Or the brown nightjar?

Do I hear or see?
Do I wake or dream?
Never you ask,
Says the changing stream.

Tavistock Goose Fair

The day my father took me to the Fair
Was just before he died of the First War.
We walked the damp, dry-leaved October air.
My father was twenty-seven and I was four.

The train was whistles and smoke and dirty steam.
I won myself a smudge of soot in the eye.
He tricked it out as we sat by a windy stream.
Farmers and gypsies were drunken-dancing by.

My dad wore his Irish cap, his riding-coat.
His boots and leggings shone as bright as a star.
He carried an ashling stick, stood soldier-straight.
The touch of his hand was strong as an iron bar.

The roundabout played 'Valencia' on the Square.
I heard the frightened geese in a wicker pen.
Out of his mouth an Indian man blew fire.
There was a smell of beer; cold taste of rain.

The cheapjacks bawled best crockery made of bone,
Solid silver spoons and cures for a cold.
My father bought a guinea for half-a-crown.
The guinea was a farthing painted gold.

Everyone else was tall. The sky went black.
My father stood me high on a drinking-trough.
I saw a man in chains escape from a sack.
I bothered in case a gypsy carried me off.

Today, I hardly remember my father's face;
Only the shine of his boot-and-legging leather
The day we walked the yellow October weather;
Only the way he strode at a soldier's pace,
The way he stood like a soldier of the line;
Only the feel of his iron hand on mine.

The Fair is still held every year at this Devonshire town on the second
Wednesday in October.

Who's That Up There?

'Who's that up there?'
Called Jinny-lie-by-the-Church.

'Didn't hear a sound
All morning,'
Said Tom Snoring.

'Nor I,'
Said Little Jack Found.

'Seeming you're dreaming,'
Grizzled old Grannie Mutton.

'Children at play!'
Yawned Ben-sleep-till-Doomsday.

'Certainly so,'
Breathed Danny Button.

Said Jinny, 'Well,
I fancy I hear a bell
And Parson Hook
Mumbling out of his book,
And feet that do tread
The green overhead.'

'Think you're right.'
Muffled Granfer Blight.
'I'm sure as sure
Someone or other,
Middle of summer,
Is coming to make
One more.'

'Ain't enough room,'
Whispered Sally Coombe.
'Best they held steady.
Bit of a squash here
Already.'

'Hope it ain't Fiddler Niall,
Him with the teeth and the smile,'
Said Long Tommy Tile.

'Or Journeyman Seth,
Hedger and ditcher,
Him with the cider
On his breath,'
Said Peter the Preacher.

'Or that Mrs Handle,
Talks nothing but scandal,
Or young Peter Blunder
With the bull-chest and the voice
Like thunder,'
Said Bessie Boyce.

'Or Jessie Priddle the teacher
– Bossy old creature –
She'd soon tell us all
What to do,'
Said Barty Blue.

'O dear!' they sighed
With a groan.

'Why can't they leave us
Alone?'
Cried Crusty-the-Baker.
'It's peaceful and easeful
We are
In God's little acre.'

Paradise

We called it Paradise: a plat of grass,
Strong weeds and wildflowers out of sight between
The broken guard-tower and the precipice
Of steps that fell down from the keep. The green
Grew higher than a child. Nobody knew
How it had got its name. To walk into
Its secrecy was to be lost from view
To all but God or some mad creature who
Had climbed the ivy to the castle top
And speer what the rest of the world could not.
See you in Paradise, we'd say. For here
Was entrance to another land, and if
No one had followed or had gone before
Its stillness was companion enough.

Today I saw it on the Castle Plan:
Close-trimmed and labelled, innocence quite gone.
Quite gone? From a washed sky the sun burned red
On green. *See you in Paradise*, I said.

Climb the Stair

Climb the stair, Katie,
Climb the stair, Paul,
The sun is down
On the orchard wall.

All through the valley
The air turns blue,
Silvers the meadow-grass
With dew.

High in the tower
The scritch owl cries,
Watching where darkest
Darkness lies.

The bats round the barnyard
Skim and stray
From last of light
To first of day.

Unseen, the water
Winds on the weir,
Sings a night-song
For all to hear.

Good night, Katie,
Good night, Paul,
Sleep till the new day
Comes to call.

Jeremiah

Jeremiah
Jumped out of the fire
Into the frying pan;
Went zig and zag
With a sausage and egg
All the way to Japan.

But when he got
To Fuji-san
And saw the mountain smoking,
'Good gracious,' said he.
'This ain't for me';
Ran all the way back to Woking.

Love Songs

Wilbur

Wilbur, Wilbur,
Your bed is made of silver,
Your sheets are Irish linen,
Your pillow soft as snow.
Wilbur, Wilbur,
The girls all look you over,
Look you up and look you down
When into town you go.

Wilbur, Wilbur,
Walking by the river,
Swifter than the sunlight
Is your glancing eye.
Wilbur, Wilbur,
You're the sweetest singer.
You've a pair of dancing legs
That money cannot buy.

Wilbur, Wilbur,
On your little finger
You wear a ring of platinum
Set with a diamond stone.
But Wilbur, Wilbur,
Now the days are colder
You go to bed at six o'clock
And lie there all alone.

Lucy Love's Song

I love a boy in Boulder,
I love a boy in Kew,
I love a boy in Bangalore
And one in Timbuktu.

I love a boy in Bari,
I love a boy in Rhyll,
I love a boy in Medicine Hat
And also in Seville.

I love a boy in Brooklyn,
I love a boy in Lille,
I love a boy in Alice Springs,
I love a boy in Kiel.

I love a boy in Ballarat,
I love a boy in Hayle,
I love a boy in Yellowknife,
I love a boy in Yale.

I love a boy in Buda,
I love a boy in Pest,
I love a boy in Trincomalee,
I love a boy in Brest.

I love a boy in Brisbane,
I love a boy in Ayr,
I love a boy in Aldershot,
I love a boy in Clare.

I love a boy in Augusta
In the State of Maine,
But the boy I love the best of all
Lives just along the lane.

Tommy Hyde

Tommy Hyde, Tommy Hyde,
What are you doing by the salt-sea side?

Picking up pebbles and smoothing sand
And writing a letter on the ocean strand.

Tommy Hyde, Tommy Hyde,
Why do you wait by the turning tide?

I'm watching for the water to rub it off the shore
And take it to my true-love in Baltimore.

Johnnie Groat Says

Johnnie Groat says my eyes are blue,
He says my hair is curled,
He says I am the prettiest maid
He saw in all the world.

    Dearest, your hair is straight as string,
    One eye is black, one brown,
    And you are the homeliest-looking girl
    Was ever in Launceston town.

Johnnie Groat says I'm smart and slim,
My hands are soft as snow,
And nobody walks as well as I
When to the fields I go.

    Sweetheart, your shift is all in rags,
    Your hands are red as kale,
    And it's well-known at sixteen stone
    You turn the miller's scale.

Johnnie Groat says my voice is sweet
As water is or wine,
And when my grannie goes up to heaven
Her pig and cot are mine.

Dear, when you walk about the wood
The birds fall down on the floor,
And your grannie of fifty years is good
For half a century more.

Then shall I not marry good Johnnie Groat
Who thinks so well of me?
And shall he not give me a fine gold ring
When he goes back to sea?

Daughter, but take the fine gold ring
And the love that's in his eye,
For the love that comes from an honest poor man
Is more than money can buy,
More than money can buy.

Rise up, Jenny

Rise up, Jenny.
Tidy your bed.
Bring the torn doll
Lies at your head.
   Not today, said Jenny.

Rise up, Jenny.
Go, milk the cow.
Feed the squabble of hens
And the black sow.
   Not today, said Jenny.

Rise up, Jenny.
Hear the school bell.
Time to read, time to count,
Time to spell.
   Not today, said Jenny.

Rise up, Jenny.
Time to cook, time to bake,
Time to wash crocks.
Time to mend, to make.
   Not today, said Jenny.

Rise up, Jenny.
Young man at the gate
Says it's you he will see
Though a year he must wait.
   Not today, said Jenny.

Rise up, Jenny.
Hear the ringing tower.
Take your veil, your white gown
And the orange flower.
   Not today, said Jenny.

My Young Man's a Cornishman

My young man's a Cornishman
He lives in Camborne town,
I met him going up the hill
As I was coming down.

His eye is bright as Dolcoath tin,
His body as china clay,
His hair is dark as Werrington Wood
Upon St Thomas's Day.

He plays the rugby football game
On Saturday afternoon,
And we shall walk on Wilsey Down
Under the bouncing moon.

My young man's a Cornishman,
Won't leave me in the lurch,
And one day we shall married be
Up to Trura church.[1]

He's bought me a ring of Cornish gold,
A belt of copper made,
At Bodmin Fair for my wedding-dress
A purse of silver paid.

[1] Truro Cathedral

And I shall give him scalded cream
And starry-gazy pie,[2]
And make him a saffron cake for tea
And a pasty for by and by.

My young man's a Cornishman,
A proper young man is he,
And a Cornish man with a Cornish maid
Is how it belongs to be.

[2] fish pie, made of pilchards. The fish are cooked whole, with the heads
piercing the crust as though gazing up to the heavens.

Take Me to the Water Fair

Take me to the Water Fair,
Row me in your boat,
Whisper with the willow tree
As down the stream we float.

The sky was cold as iron
When we set off from land,
But soon, you say, a day will come
With flowers on either hand.

Let me lie upon your arm
As on the flood we slide
And watch the shining fishes play
Swiftly our boat beside.

And here the lilies lean upon
The waters as we pass,
And there the munching cattle swim
Deep in the meadow grass.

As high above the chestnut burns
Its candles on the sky
You say that summer cannot end –
And you will never lie.

If You Should Go to Caistor Town

If you should go to Caistor town
    Where my true-love has gone,
Ask her why she went away
    And left me here alone.

She said the Caistor sky was blue,
    The wind was never cold,
The pavements were all made of pearl,
    The young were never old.

Never a word she told me more
    But when the year was fled,
Upon a bed of brightest earth
    She laid her gentle head.

When I went up to Caistor
  My suit was made of black,
And all her words like summer birds
  Upon the air came back.

  O when I went to Caistor
    With ice the sky was sown,
  And all the streets were chill and grey
    And they were made of stone.

Rebekah

Rebekah, Rebekah,
Wake up from your sleep,
The cattle are thirsty
And so are the sheep
That come with the evening
Down from the high fell
To drink the sweet water
Of Paradise Well.

Rebekah, Rebekah,
The spring rises free
But the well it is locked
And you have the key,
And the sheep and the cattle
Rebekah, are dry
And would drink of the water.
And so would I.

Don't Cry, Sally

Don't cry, Sally,
Don't cry, Sue,
Don't tell your mammy
You don't know what to do.

Though on your cheek
The tears run down,
Put on your dancing shoes,
Skip round the town.

Don't cry, Dinah,
Don't cry, Dee,
There's many another
Swims in the sea.

Bind up your hair,
Sing and play,
Tomorrow is another
Dancing day.

Don't cry, Amabel,
Don't cry, Ann,
Now you know who's
My fancy man.

They say he's a shuffling
Scamping one,
But I know he'll love me
Till the world is done.

Early in the morning
When the songbirds sing
You shall hear
The church bells ring.

It's goodbye pretty,
It's goodbye plain,
You never shall see
My face again.

Serena

Serena lies under the waterfall
In the blue sound of the sea.
Soft and sweet I hear her sing
By the feathery tamarisk tree,
Its flowers pink, its flowers white,
She sings all through the moonwashed night.
Who do you sing for, Serena?
            Teach your song to me.

Do you sing for the healthy farmer
Or the sailor on the quay?
Is it for Tom the Drover
Or the lawyer with his fee?
Do you sing for the pedlar with his pack,
Or Schoolie, or Silly Strong-Arm Jack?
Who do you sing for, Serena?
            Teach your song to me.

Do you sing your song for a beggar
Or the banker with fortunes three?
Is it he who swims the valley stream
Or the climber on the scree?
Is your song for the soldier on the square,
The boy on the hunter, the boy in the air?
'For none of you,' says Serena.
            'Nor shall it ever be.'

Johnny Come Over the Water

Johnny come over the water
And make the sun shine through.
Johnny come over the water
And paint the sky with blue.

Cover the field and the meadow
With flowers of red and gold
And cover with leaves the simple trees
That stand so bare and cold.

Johnny come over the water,
Turn the white grass to hay.
It's winter, winter all the year
Since you went away.

When I Was a Hundred and Twenty-six

When I was a hundred and twenty-six
And you were a hundred and four
What fun, my dearest dear, we had
At the back of the Co-op store.
It was all such a very long time ago
That it seems just like a dream
In the days when you called me your own Rich Tea
And you were my Custard Cream.

Such joys we knew with those dinners *à deux*
At the bottom of the parking lot
On roasted gnu and buffalo stew
And Tandoori chicken in a pot.
Such songs, my love, we used to sing
Till the stars had lost their shine,
And the bells of heaven rang ding, ding, ding
And the neighbours rang 999.

When I was a hundred and twenty-six
And you were a hundred and four
We thought love's cherry would last a very
Long time, and then some more.
But days are fleet when ways are sweet
As the honey in a hive –
And I am a hundred and twenty-seven
And you are a hundred and five.

Give Me a House

Give me a house, said Polly.
Give me land, said Hugh.
Give me the moon, said Sadie.
Give me the sun, said Sue.

Give me a horse, said Rollo.
Give me a hound, said Joe.
Give me fine linen, said Sarah.
Give me silk, said Flo.

Give me a mountain, said Kirsty.
Give me a valley, said Jim.
Give me a river, said Dodo.
Give me the sky, said Tim.

Give me the ocean, said Adam.
Give me a ship, said Hal.
Give me a kingdom, said Rory.
Give me a crown, said Sal.

Give me gold, said Peter.
Give me silver, said Paul.
Give me love, said Jenny,
Or nothing at all.

Season and Festival

Here We Go Round the Round House

Here we go round the Round House
In the month of one,
Looking to the eastward
For the springing sun.
The sky is made of ashes,
The trees are made of bone,
And all the water in the well
Is stubborn as a stone.

Here we go round the Round House
In the month of two,
Waiting for the weather
To thaw my dancing shoe.
In St Thomas River
Hide the freckled trout,
But for dinner on Friday
I shall pull one out.

Here we go round the Round House
In the month of three,
Listening for the bumble
Of the humble-bee.
The light is growing longer,
The geese begin to lay,
The song-thrush in the churchyard
Charms the cold away.

Here we go round the Round House
In the month of four,
Watching a couple dressed in green
Dancing through the door.
One wears a wreath of myrtle,
Another, buds of thorn:
God grant that all men's children
Be as sweetly born.

Here we go round the Round House
In the month of five,
Waiting for the summer
To tell us we're alive.
All round the country
The warm seas flow,
The devil's on an ice-cap
Melting with the snow.

Here we go round the Round House
In the month of six;
High in the tower
The town clock ticks.
Hear the black quarter-jacks
Beat the noon bell;
They say the day is half away
And the year as well.

Here we go round the Round House
In the month of seven,
The river running thirsty
From Cornwall to Devon.
The sun is on the hedgerow,
The cattle in the stream,
And one will give us strawberries
And one will give us cream.

Here we go round the Round House
In the month of eight,
Hoping that for harvest
We shall never wait.
Slyly the sunshine
Butters up the bread
To bear us through the winter
When the light is dead.

Here we go round the Round House
In the month of nine,
Watching the orchard apple
Turning into wine.
The day after tomorrow
I'll take one from the tree
And pray the worm will do no harm
If it comes close to me.

Here we go round the Round House
In the month of ten,
While the cattle winter
In the farmer's pen.
Thick the leaves are lying
On the coppice floor;
Such a coat against the cold
Never a body wore.

Here we go round the Round House
In the month of eleven,
The sea-birds swiftly flying
To the coast of heaven.
The plough is in the furrow,
The boat is on the strand;
May I be fed on fish and bread
While water lies on land.

Here we go round the Round House
In the month of twelve,
The hedgers break the briar
And the ditchers delve.
As we go round the Round House
May the moon and sun
Guide us to tomorrow
And the month of one:
And life be never done.

The Round House, c.1830, is built over a broken market cross at
Launceston, in Cornwall.

In Canada

Walking down Beaver
I heard the stone river
Snap like a string.
Spring! you say. It is spring!

Walking down Buffalo
See where ice crystals, snow
Lift off brown grass.
Pass, summer, pass!

Walking down Wolf
Watch a single gold leaf
Sink and lie still.
Fall! you say. Fall!

Walking down Bear
I see afternoon air
Turn grey, turn blear.
Winter, you say, is here!

Walking down Beaver
Watch sky, tree uncover
Secret green, secret blue.
Still the great wheel turns true!

The streets of the Canadian town of Banff, in the Rocky Mountains, are
named after various native animals.

Logs of Wood

When in the summer sky the sun
Hung like a golden ball,
John Willy from the Workhouse came
And loudly he would bawl:

Wood! Wood! Logs of wood
To keep out the cold!
Shan't be round tomorrow!
They all must be sold!

But O the sky was shining blue
And green was the spray.
It seemed as if the easy days
Would never pass away.

And when John Willy came to town
The laughter it would start,
And we would smile as he went by
Pushing his wooden cart.

John Willy, I can see you still
Coming down Tower Street,
Your pointed nose, your cast-off clothes,
Your Charlie Chaplin feet.

And like the prophet you would stand
Calling loud and long,
But there were few who listened to
The story of your song.

Wood! Wood! Logs of wood
To keep out the cold!
Shan't be round tomorrow!
They all must be sold!

But now the snow is on the hill,
The ice is on the plain,
And dark as dark a shadow falls
Across my window-pane.

Tomorrow, ah tomorrow –
That name I did not fear
Until Tomorrow came and said,
Good morrow. I am here.

At Candlemas

'If Candlemas be fine and clear
There'll be two winters in that year';

But all the day the drumming sun
Brazened it out that spring had come,

And the tall elder on the scene
Unfolded the first leaves of green.

But when another morning came
With frost, as Candlemas with flame,

The sky was steel, there was no sun,
The elder leaves were dead and gone.

Out of a cold and crusted eye
The stiff pond stared up at the sky,

And on the scarcely breathing earth
A killing wind fell from the north;

But still within the elder tree
The strong sap rose, though none could see.

Candlemas Day is on 2 February.

Tomorrow is Simnel Sunday

Tomorrow is Simnel Sunday
And homeward I shall steer
And I must bake a simnel cake
For my mother dear.

I'll fetch me almonds, cherries,
The finest in the land,
I'll fetch me salt, I'll fetch me spice,
I'll fetch me marzipan.

With milk and eggs and butter
And flour as fair as snow
And raisins sweet and candied treat
I'll set it all to go.

And I shall search for violets
That scent the homeward way
For tomorrow is Simnel Sunday
And it is Mothering Day.

Simnel (or Mothering) Sunday is the fourth Sunday in Lent. Following an old custom, children visited their parents for the day and took gifts of cake and flowers.

Frost on the Flower

Frost on the flower,
Leaf and frond,
Snow on the field-path,
Ice on the pond.

Out of the east
A white wind comes.
Hail on the rooftop
Kettledrums.

Snow-fog wanders
Hollow and hill.
Along the valley
The stream is still.

Thunder and lightning.
Down slaps the rain.
No doubt about it.
Summer again.

Count Pollen

Count Pollen walked his English land
Under the summer blue.
'County, good day to you!' I cried.
        Tchoo! said the Count. *A-tchoo!*

The noon was bright, a thirsty sun
Had swallowed up the dew.
'I trust I find you well?' I asked.
        Tchoo! said the Count. *A-tchoo!*

The softest breezes from the south
Among the grasses blew.
'How sweet,' I called, 'the summer air!'
        Tchoo! said the Count. *A-tchoo!*

Along the valley floor the stream
Its silver waters drew.
'Is good to be alive!' I cried.
        Tchoo! said the Count. *A-tchoo!*

'In all of England,' I remarked,
'Was never such a view –
Ah, do you not agree, my Lord?'
        Tchoo! said the Count. *A-tchoo!*

'There's never a one who does not wish
He was,' I said, 'as you.
But why the tears upon your cheek?'
        Tchoo! said the Count. *A-tchoo!*

Why?

Why do you turn your head, Susanna,
And why do you swim your eye?
It's only the children on Bellman Street
Calling, *A penny for the guy!*

Why do you look away, Susanna,
As the children wheel him by?
It's only a dummy in an old top-hat
And a fancy jacket and tie.

Why do you take my hand, Susanna,
As the pointing flames jump high?
It's only a bundle of sacking and straw.
Nobody's going to die.

Why is your cheek so pale, Susanna,
As the whizzbangs flash and fly?
It's nothing but a rummage of paper and rag
Strapped to a stick you spy.

Why do you say you hear, Susanna,
The sound of a last, long sigh?
And why do you say it won't leave your head
No matter how hard you try?

Best let me take you home, Susanna.
Best on your bed to lie.
It's only a dummy in an old top-hat.
Nobody's going to die.

Round the Corner Comes Jack Fall

Round the corner comes Jack Fall,
Dressed in yellow, dressed in brown.
'Goodbye, summer,' hear him call
As he wanders through the town.

'Give her a kiss and wish her well,
Give her a gold and silver chain.
Tell her you love her,' said Jack Fall.
'And bring her back this way again.'

On St Catherine's Day

We are the Workhouse children,
Maids dressed in white,
Our gowns are trimmed with ribbon,
With flowers our hair is bright.

Before us walks the Master
With sure and steady tread,
And here is the tallest maid of all
A gilt crown on her head.

She bears in her hand a sceptre
Of yellow wood and tin,
And in the other a distaff
With which we may spin.

Pray give to us your ha'pennies
And give your farthings too,
That we may buy the wheels and reels
Our finest work to do.

On this day good St Catherine
To the sharp wheel has been,
Catherine, Saint of Spinners,
Catherine our Queen.

Today we shall eat rump steak
And we shall dance and game,
But the day is short and the year is long
Before it comes again.

We stand in church for the Parson,
We sit both straight and tall
As do the little stone children
That are beside the wall.

Our faces are white as paper,
Our hands are made of bone,
We may not speak the truth with our tongues
But with our eyes alone.

Though the Workhouse wall is broken,
With truest eye and clear
Watch for the Workhouse children,
For we are always here.

In Victorian times, girls living in the local Workhouse were led in procession round the town by the Workhouse Master. They stopped and sang before the houses of important local people, and were later given money, a special dinner and tea, and were allowed to play games in the evening. This all took place on 25 November, the Feast Day of the martyred St Catherine of Alexandria, who in the fourth century had been tortured on a spiked wheel (the Catherine wheel). St Catherine is the patron saint of young girls, and also of all whose work is connected with the wheel, such as spinners, millers and wheelwrights. Females in the old Workhouses were employed on spinning.

At Nine of the Night I Opened My Door

At nine of the night I opened my door
That stands midway between moor and moor,
And all around me, silver-bright,
I saw that the world had turned to white.

Thick was the snow on field and hedge
And vanished was the river-sedge,
Where winter skilfully had wound
A shining scarf without a sound.

And as I stood and gazed my fill
A stable-boy came down the hill.
With every step I saw him take
Flew at his heel a puff of flake.

His brow was whiter than the hoar,
A beard of freshest snow he wore,
And round about him, snowflake starred,
A red horse-blanket from the yard.

In a red cloak I saw him go,
His back was bent, his step was slow,
And as he laboured through the cold
He seemed a hundred winters old.

I stood and watched the snowy head,
The whiskers white, the cloak of red.
'A Merry Christmas!' I heard him cry.
'The same to you, old friend,' said I.

Tam Snow
(to Kaye Webb)

Who in the white wood
Barefoot, ice-fingered,
Runs to and fro?
> *Tam Snow.*

Who, soft as a ghost,
Falls on our house to strike
Blow after blow?
> *Tam Snow.*

Who with a touch of the hand
Stills the world's sound
In its flow?
> *Tam Snow.*

Who holds to our side,
Though as friend or as foe
We never may know?
> *Tam Snow.*

Who hides in the hedge
After thaw, waits for more
Of his kind to show?
> *Tam Snow.*

Who is the guest
First we welcome, then
Long to see go?
> *Tam Snow.*

Giglets' Market

Tomorrow at Giglets' Market
I'll find a farmer who
Will take me as a hired man
For fifty weeks and two.

Tomorrow at Giglets' Market
I shall never be late
For I must go to market
To meet me with a mate.

I shall wear my Sunday suit,
My good cap on my head
And at my throat a handkerchief
Of yellow and of red.

In my right hand an oak stick
Ribboned with a bow,
And in my left I'll bear a pinch
Of holly and mistletoe.

I shall stand up straight and strong
And I shall never fear
To find a farmer who shall pay
Me ten gold pounds a year.

I'll stroll the setts and cobbles round,
I'll give the girls the eye
And with my besten Sunday boots
I'll make the sparks to fly.

And I shall meet a maid before
The ending of the day
And on the swings and roundabouts
We'll ride the hours away.

And when the fair is over
I'll ask her fresh and fine,
I'll ask her mammy, I'll ask her daddy
If I may call her mine.

She's certain sure to take me
And give to me her hand,
For I am a Cornish country boy
And I work the Cornish land.

When I was a boy in my home town of Launceston, Giglets' Market was held on the first Saturday after Christmas. It was a hiring-fair, to which farm-workers (female as well as male) came if they were seeking fresh employment. Traditionally it was also the day when young men and women searched for partners.

They're Fetching in Ivy and Holly

'They're fetching in ivy and holly
And putting it this way and that.
I simply can't think of the reason,'
Said Si-Si the Siamese cat.

'They're pinning up lanterns and streamers.
There's mistletoe over the door.
They've brought in a tree from the garden.
I do wish I knew what it's for.

'It's covered with little glass candles
That go on and off without stop.
They've put it to stand in a corner
And tied up a fairy on top.

'They're stringing bright cards by the dozen
And letting them hang in a row.
Some people outside in the roadway
Are singing a song in the snow.

'I saw all the children write letters
And – I'm not at all sure this was wise –
They posted each one *up the chimney*.
I couldn't believe my own eyes.

'What on earth, in the middle of winter,
Does the family think it is at?
Won't somebody please come and tell me?'
Said Si-Si the Siamese cat.

Parson's Lea

That Christmas we went carolling
Over at Parson's Lea:
Barnaby Bly, Sam and Sal Spry,
Mickey McGee and me.

Said Sammy, 'We're sure of a dollar
If we sing out sweet and fine,
And cakes and pies to dazzle your eyes
And glasses of home-made wine!'

So quiet we came to Parson's Lea
And nobody heard us come.
The trees they leaned and the scritch-owl screamed
And my heart began to drum.

Up we went to Parson's Lea
And never a star did shine,
By the graveyard wall and the tower tall
And the church clock telling nine.

We started on *Good King Wenceslas*
But Barnaby pitched it high
And Sally she wriggled and Sammy he giggled
And Mickey began to cry.

Down came a bucket of water
That wetted us to the skin,
And that was our fee at Parson's Lea
And nobody asked us in.

As we went home by the Ridgeway
Barney and Mick turned blue
And Sal she quivered and Sam he bivered
And I was shivering too,

When out of her cottage doorway
There looked old Jennifer Starr.
'Come in,' she said, 'for it's half of dead
And cold and tired you are.

'Sit yourselves down by the fireside
And give yourselves a bake.'
And as soon as we sat by Tom the cat
She brought out *a Christmas cake*.

She gave to us each an orange,
A drink that was hot and neat,
And a little man made of marzipan –
The best we ever did eat.

'Will you sing *King Wenceslas*?' she said.
'There's nothing that I'd like more!'
And for Jennifer Starr we sang better by far
Than ever we sang before.

Now Jenny has slept in her green bed
Fifty years and ten,
But I see her clear with her Christmas cheer
As the day I saw her then.

And Barnaby Bly is a banker,
Sammy's as skint as Job,
And Mickey McGee ran off to sea
And was seven times round the globe.

Sally she married a soldier
Came from the USA
And not a word has one of us heard
From Sal since she went away.

But in the dark of winter
When Christmas comes again,
Every year I'm certain sure
We remember it plain as plain –

Barnaby Bly, Sam and Sal Spry,
Mickey McGee and me:
The Christmas we went carolling
Over at Parson's Lea.

A Song of Truth

When Christ the Lord of Heaven was born
Cold was the land.
His mother saw along the road
A fig-tree stand.
'Good Mary, leave the figs to grow
For we have thirty miles to go.
The hour is late.'

Mary came near unto the town.
Stayed at a door.
Said to the little farmer, 'Pray
Let us stay here.
Not for myself these words I make
But for an infant child's sake.
The night is chill.'

The farmer opened up his barn.
Bade them go in.
When half the winter night had gone
Came there again.
'Where you are from in this wide world,
And are not killed by winter cold,
I cannot tell.'

The farmer came into his house
The barn beside.
'Rise up, dear wife,' he cried, 'and may
Best fire be made
That these poor travellers are warm
And safe from wind and weather's harm
Here at our hearth.'

Smiling, Mary then entered in
The farmhouse door;
Also her good and gentle man
That self-same hour
Drew from his pack a crock of tin.
With snow the young child filled it fine,
And it was flour.

Crystals of ice he placed therein
As sugar rare
And water that white milk should be
Both fresh and fair.
Over the flame they hung the crock,
And such soft sweetness did they cook,
Was finest pap.

Of wooden chip the good man carved
With homely blade
A spoon that was of ivory
And diamond made.
And now the child does Mary sweet
Give of the pap that He may eat:
Jesus His name.

Translated from the German

The Animals' Carol

Christus natus est! the cock   Christ is born
Carols on the morning dark.

Quando? croaks the raven stiff,   When?
Freezing on the broken cliff.

Hoc nocte, replies the crow,   This night
Beating high above the snow.

Ubi? Ubi? booms the ox   Where?
From its cavern in the rocks.

Bethlehem, then bleats the sheep,   Bethlehem
Huddled on the winter steep.

Quomodo? the brown hare clicks,   How?
Chattering among the sticks.

Humiliter, the careful wren   Humbly
Thrills upon the cold hedge-stone.

Cur? Cur? sounds the coot   Why?
By the iron river-root.

Propter homines, the thrush   For the sake of
Sings on the sharp holly-bush.   man

Cui? Cui? rings the chough   To whom?
On the strong, sea-haunted bluff.

Mary! Mary! calls the lamb   Mary
From the quiet of the womb.

Praeterea ex quo? cries   Who else?
The woodpecker to pallid skies.

Joseph, breathes the heavy shire,   Joseph
Warming in its own blood-fire.

Ultime ex quo? the owl   Who above all?
Solemnly begins to call.

De Deo, the little stare   Of God
Whistles on the hardening air.

Pridem? Pridem? the jack snipe   Long ago?
From the harsh grass starts to pipe.

Sic et non, answers the fox,
Tiptoeing the bitter lough.

Yes and no

Quomodo hoc scire potest?
Boldly flutes the robin redbreast.

How do I know this?

Illo in eandem, squeaks
The mouse within the barley-sack.

By going there

Quae sarcinae? asks the daw,
Swaggering from head to claw.

What luggage?

Nulla res, replies the ass,
Bearing on its back the Cross.

None

Quantum pecuniae? shrills
The wandering gull about the hills.

How much money?

Ne nummum quidem, the rook
Caws across the rigid brook.

Not a penny

Nulla resne? barks the dog   Nothing at all?
By the crumbling fire-log.

Nil nisi cor amans, the dove   Only a loving
Murmurs from its house of love.   heart

Gloria in Excelsis! Then
Man is God, and God is Man.

Christmas at Les Baux

Angels, under elm and lotus
On St Vincent Square
Adjust a drifted wing, a halo.
Fix their gold hair.

Shepherds, caped and scarved for winter
From field are come;
Gather at the church door, sounding
Squealing fife, the drum.

See the small cart hung with greening
Drawn by the ram;
Safe in straw and soft hay lying
The new-born lamb.

Now among the winking candles,
Shadowed stone and painted glass
Breaks the Christmas hymn at midnight
As they pass.

Fierce the moonlight, fierce the starlight
Burn on crag and scree.
Deep below, the river reaches
For the sea.

In the town of rock, of ruin
Slung between the sky, the plain,
Hear the voicing, the rejoicing.
Christ is born again.

The ceremony described here still takes place on Christmas Eve in the
French hill-town of Les Baux-en-Provence.

Angels' Song

First angel	Fear not, shepherds, for I bring Tidings of a new-born King – Not in castle, not in keep, Nor in tower strong and steep. Not in manor-house or hall, But a humble ox's stall.
Second angel	Underneath a standing star And where sheep and cattle are, In a bed of straw and hay God's own Son is born this day. If to Bethlehem you go, This the truth you soon shall know.
Third angel	And as signal and as sign, Sure as all the stars that shine, You shall find him, shepherds all, Swaddled in a baby-shawl; And the joyful news will share With good people everywhere.
Second angel	Therefore, listen as we cry:
Three angels	Glory be to God on high, And his gifts of love and peace To his people never cease.

From the play *The Gift of a Lamb*

Driving Home

Driving home, in wrong weather,
Half-melted stars adrift
In a warmth of sky, the tin voice
Of the car radio sprinkling
Music for Spanish guitar,
I had forgotten, for some reason,
Time, place and season.

Then, suddenly, the church:
Lit granite lantern.
Coloured glass saints pointing
Stiff arms to pray or praise.
Over its ragged screen
Of elm, yew, oak,
The tower spoke.

As if at the push of dark
The door unclosed.
Men, women, children
In smiling light
Streamed a thin path between
Tomb and long-planted stone.
Headed for home.

Above, six bells (one cracked)
Thumped down the scale.
'Merry Christmas!' Tom, Jack
And Maisie called.
'Don't seem like Christmas.
More like Midsummer,'
They grinned one to another.

'Every day Christmas Day!'
They smelt of whisky and tobacco.
Climbed into the bent, half-spent van,
Making for Moor Farm
As I wondered what,
In all that Mediterranean air,
They should discover there.

Mary's Song

Sleep, King Jesus,
Your royal bed
Is made of hay
In a cattle-shed.
Sleep, King Jesus,
Do not fear,
Joseph is watching
And waiting near.

Warm in the wintry air
You lie,
The ox and the donkey
Standing by.
With summer eyes
They seem to say:
Welcome, Jesus,
On Christmas Day!

Sleep, King Jesus:
Your diamond crown
High in the sky
Where the stars look down.
Let your reign
Of love begin,
That all the world
May enter in.

From the play *The Gift of a Lamb*

Legend

Snow-blind the meadow; chiming ice
Struck at the wasted water's rim.
An infant in a stable lay.
A child watched for a sight of Him.

'I would have brought spring flowers,' she said.
'But where I wandered none did grow.'
Young Gabriel smiled, opened his hand,
And blossoms pierced the sudden snow.

She plucked the gold, the red, the green,
And with a garland entered in.
'What is your name?' Young Gabriel said.
The maid she answered, 'Magdalene.'

Christmas Pudding

Christmas pudding,
    Christmas cracker,
Christmas turkey,
    Christmas tree,
They all sat down together
    And were sad as sad could be
For Christmas-time was coming
    And they felt for certain sure
By Christmas night things wouldn't quite
    Be as they were before.

'I wish you hadn't told me,'
    The Christmas pudding said,
'They'll boil me in a pan and stick
    Some holly in my head,
And after Christmas dinner
    (This is the bit I hate)
There's not a plum or pudding crumb
    On anybody's plate.'

'It's clear enough,' the turkey huffed,
    'For anyone to see
When I say *Hobble! Gobble!*
    I don't mean gobble me.
But bless my feathers, bless my beak,
    When Christmas Day has flown,
I've heard what's left of this poor bird
    Is only skin and bone.'

'I can't deny,' the cracker cried,
    'I'm feeling rather blue
That all this red and green and gold
    Will soon be torn in two.
As for the rest, I must confess,
    It gives me such a pang
To know that by this time next week
    I've gone off with a bang.'

'Dear me,' then said the Christmas tree,
    'It makes me want to blub.
I hear they're going to pull me up
    And stand me in a tub.
And when the party's over
    And my needles dropped and dead,
They'll throw me on the rubbish heap
    Behind the garden shed.'

Said the turkey to the pudding
    And the cracker and the tree,
'Though Christmas is a jolly time
    And fills most folk with glee,
It's something rather different
    For you, my friends, and me –
And just what must become of us
    Is all too plain to see.'

So the cracker and the turkey
    And the pudding and the tree
They all ran off together
    Over land and over sea.
They crossed the silver river
    And they crossed the snowy plain
And they crossed the ragged mountain
    And were never seen again.

And north or south or east or west
    In air or on the ground,
There's never been a sign of them
    And never been a sound
Since they crept across the meadow
    And they leapt across the lea,
Happy pudding,
           Happy cracker,
Happy turkey,
           Happy tree.

Salt-sea and Shore

Morwenstow

Where do you come from, sea,
To the sharp Cornish shore,
Leaping up to the raven's crag?
    From Labrador.

Do you grow tired, sea?
Are you weary ever
When the storms burst over your head?
    Never.

Are you hard as a diamond, sea,
As iron, as oak?
Are you stronger than flint or steel?
    And the lightning stroke.

Ten thousand years and more, sea,
You have gobbled your fill,
Swallowing stone and slate!
    I am hungry still.

When will you rest, sea?
    *When moon and sun
    Ride only fields of salt water
    And the land is gone.*

The Merrymaid

Robert Stephen Hawker,
Vicar of Morwenstow,
Dressed himself in a merrymaid skin,
Swam out with the flow.

And with a coral-branch he combed
His hair so limp and long,
And high in a screamy voice he sang
A sea-weedy sort of song.

From near and far the people came
To walk on the cliff-top green,
For none had heard a merrymaid sing
Nor ever a merrymaid seen.

The first night that the merrymaid sang
The moon was white as bone,
And sad was the song they heard her sing
As she sat on a slippery stone.

The second night that the merrymaid sang
The moon was beaming brass,
And sweet was the song they heard her sing
As she gazed in her looking-glass.

The third night that the merrymaid sang
The moon was thin and pale,
And when she had sung her sweet-sad song
She stood up straight on her tail.

As stiff as a soldier she stood up
In a phosphorescent sheen,
And with arms straight down by her sides she sang
'God Save our Gracious Queen.'

Then into the dancing sea she dove
To the running billows' roar,
And vanished beneath the wheeling waves
And was seen on the coast no more.

Robert Stephen Hawker,
Vicar of Morwenstow,
Stripped himself of the merrymaid skin
He wore from top to toe.

And the Vicar he smiled and pondered
As he went upstairs to bed
On the gullibility of man,
And sadly he shook his head.

In Cornwall, a mermaid is called a merrymaid. The poet Robert Stephen
Hawker (1803–75) was Vicar of Morwenstow, on the north coast of Cornwall, from 1834. His best-known ballad is 'And shall Trelawny die?'.

John Polruddon

John Polruddon
All of a sudden
Went out of his house one night,
  When a privateer
  Came sailing near
  Under his window-light.

They saw his jugs
His plates and mugs
His hearth as bright as brass,
  His gews and gaws
  And kicks and shaws
  All through their spying glass.

They saw his wine
His silver shine
They heard his fiddlers play.
  Tonight, they said,
  Out of his bed
  Polruddon we'll take away.

And from a skiff
They climbed the cliff
And crossed the salt-wet lawn,
        And as they crept
        Polruddon slept
        The night away to dawn.

In air or ground
What is that sound?
Polruddon said, and stirred.
        They breathed, Be still,
        It was the shrill
        Of the scritch-owl you heard.

O yet again
I hear it plain,
But do I wake or dream?
        In morning's fog
        The otter-dog
        Is whistling by the stream.

Now from the sea
What comes for me
Beneath my window dark?
        Lie still, my dear,
        All that you hear
        Is the red fox's bark.

Swift from his bed
Polruddon was sped
Before the day was white,
    And head and feet
    Wrapped in a sheet
    They bore him down the height.

And never more
Through his own door
Polruddon went nor came;
    Though many a tide
    Has turned beside
    The cliff that bears his name.

On stone and brick
Was ivy thick,
And the grey roof was thin,
    And winter's gale
    With fists of hail
    Broke all the windows in.

The chimney-crown
It tumbled down
And up grew the green,
    Till on the cliff
    It was as if
    A house had never been.

But when the moon
Swims late or soon
Across St Austell Bay,
    What sight, what sound
    Haunts air and ground
    Where once Polruddon lay?

It is the high
White scritch-owl's cry,
The fox as dark as blood,
    And on the hill
    The otter still
    Whistles beside the flood.

John Polruddon's house was on the cliff over Pentewan, in South Cornwall.
The story of his disappearance dates from early Tudor times.

Tell Me, Tell Me, Sarah Jane

Tell me, tell me, Sarah Jane,
   Tell me, dearest daughter,
Why are you holding in your hand
   A thimbleful of water?
Why do you hold it to your eye
   And gaze both late and soon
From early morning light until
   The rising of the moon?

Mother, I hear the mermaids cry,
   I hear the mermen sing,
And I can see the sailing-ships
   All made of sticks and string.
And I can see the jumping fish,
   The whales that fall and rise
And swim about the waterspout
   That swarms up to the skies.

Tell me, tell me, Sarah Jane,
   Tell your darling mother,
Why do you walk beside the tide
   As though you loved none other?
Why do you listen to a shell
   And watch the billows curl,
And throw away your diamond ring
   And wear instead the pearl?

Mother, I hear the water
   Beneath the headland pinned,
And I can see the sea-gull
   Sliding down the wind.
I taste the salt upon my tongue
   As sweet as sweet can be.

Tell me, my dear, whose voice you hear?

It is the sea, the sea.

Nicholas Naylor

Nicholas Naylor
The deep-blue sailor
Sailed the sea
As a master-tailor.

He sewed for the Captain,
He sewed for the crew,
He sewed up the kit-bags
And hammocks too.

He sewed up a serpent,
He sewed up a shark,
He sewed up a sailor
In a bag of dark.

How do you like
Your work, master-tailor?
'So, so, so,'
Said Nicholas Naylor.

What Sailors Say

Whistle in calm, the wind shall wail.
Whistle in breeze shall bring a gale.

Priest nor parson ship-board tread.
These are buriers of the dead.

Sure is he from wind and weather
If he wear the wild wren's feather.

Flowers fresh upon the blue,
Ship is lost and all her crew.

Carry a maid against the swell
She shall keep and guard you well.

The carving of a woman as a figurehead over the cutwater of a ship was believed to be a charm against severe storms.

Dawn at Ballintoy

At Ballintoy, at Ballintoy
From dusk until the light of day
Upon the height an eye of white
Opens upon the moving bay.

And now it blinks, and now it winks,
That ships and sailors passing by
May know the ragged cliff that climbs
Between the waters and the sky.

A sea-bird hazards a first flight.
The sky burns blue, the sky burns free
As Ballintoy puts on the day
Beside the sounding of the sea.

Three Green Sailors

Three green sailors
Went to sea
In a sailing ship
Called *The Flying Flea*.
Their caps were round,
Their shirts were square,
Their trousers were rolled
And their feet were bare.
One wore a pigtail,
One wore a patch,
One wore ear-rings
That never did match.
One chewed baccy,
One chewed cake,
One chewed a pennyworth
Of two-eyed steak.[1]
One danced to,
One danced fro
And the other sang the shanty
Haul Away Joe.

[1] sailors' slang for a bloater or a kipper

They cried 'Belay!'
They called 'Avast!'
They hoisted the sail
To the top of the mast.
They cast off aft,
They cast off fore
And away they sailed
From the steady shore.
'There's never a doubt,'
Said the sailors three,
'That *this* is the life
For the likes of we!'

But soon it was clear
As clear could be
Three green sailors
Were all at sea:
For nothing they knew
Of star or sun
And nothing of nav-i-
Ga-ti-on,
And they'd no idea
(For they'd never been taught)
Which was starboard
And which was port.
They never did compass
Nor chart possess

Nor a lamp nor a rocket
For an SOS.
But three green sailors
Thought it a ball
And weren't in the least
Bit troubled at all.

The sea rose up,
The light grew thin
And the tide it turned them
Out and in.
The winds blew high
As about they spun
And the thunder sounded
Like a gun.
The Flying Flea
Through the waves it flew
And sometimes *under*
The water too.
In ocean salt,
In ocean cold,
The Flying Flea
It rocked and rolled.

It shook from stem
To stern until
Three green sailors
Were greener still.
'Dear us!' they cried
And 'Help!' they roared
As the wind it whined
And the water poured.
'It's a shock,' they said,
'To our systems three
How quickly the weather
May change at sea.
Not a minute ago
The sky looked great
And now we're in the middle
Of a gale (force 8).
And another fact
We just can't skip:
We don't know a THING
About seamanship.'
So they wept, they cried
And they went all numb
And they felt their very
Last hour had come.

But old King Neptune
Down below
Heard them sobbing
Like billy-o.
He smiled a smile,
He winked an eye
And he said, 'I'll give them
One more try,
For sure as a pound
Is a hundred pence
Another time
They'll show more sense
And I've led those lubbers
Such a dance
I think they deserve
Another chance.
But before again
They take to the sea
They really must learn
A thing or three,
For those who sail
The mighty blue
Should be skilled as seamen
Through and through.
They must learn the trade
From a to zee
Or they'll all end up
Down here with me.'

And now with a blow
Of his salt-sea hand
He washed the good ship
Back to land
And three green sailors
Came ashore
Wiser by far
Than they were before.
'O never,' they said,
'Will we sail the brine
In weather that's foul
Or weather that's fine
Till we learn as well
As well can be
The ways of a sailor,
A ship and the sea.'

And with knees of jelly
And a wavery tread
Each went home
To his own sweet bed.
And Neptune laughed
On the ocean floor
And he stirred the waters
Just once more.
He stirred the waters,
He sang a salt rhyme
And he stirred the waters
One more time,
For he never will tire,
He never will sleep:
Neptune, Neptune,
King of the Deep.

Dan Dory

Today I saw Dan Dory
Walking out of the sea.
'Did you tell the world my story?'
Dan said to me.

Salt glittered on his breast, his fingers.
Drops of gold fell from his hair.
The look in his eye was sapphire-bright
As he stood there.

'Your head is white,' said Dan Dory.
'Trenched your face, your hand.
And why do you walk to greet me
So slowly across the sand?'

'I watched you held, Dan Dory,
In ocean fast.
Thirty, no, forty years ago
I saw you last.

'And now I see you older
By not a second's stroke
Than when the sun raged overhead
And the sea was flame, was smoke.'

'Did you tell the world my story?'
I heard him say.
'And for the unwisdom of the old
Do the young still pay?'

'Still spins the water and the land,'
I said, 'as yesterday' –
And leaned to take his hand. But he
Had vanished away.

A Mermaid at Zennor

A mermaid at Zennor
Climbed out of the sea
By the seething Zennor shore.
Her gown was silver,
Her gown was gold
And a crown of pearl she wore,
She wore,
A crown of pearl she wore.

The Zennor bay
Burned peacock-blue,
White was the Zennor sand
Where she came up
By Zennor Head,
Comb in her crystal hand,
Her hand,
Comb in her crystal hand.

She stood before
The great church door
That open was and wide.
She gazed into
The mirror true
She carried at her side,
Her side,
She carried at her side.

Now Zennor men
Do love to sing
Their songs both great and small,
And Sampson Scown
The Squire's son
Sang sweetest of them all,
Them all,
Sang sweetest of them all.

The mermaid stepped
Out of the sun
And slowly entered in,
Her purpose fell
By charm or spell
Young Sampson for to win,
To win,
Young Sampson for to win.

And in a sea-deep
Tongue she sang
A song that none
Had known,
And choir and congregation stood
As they were made of stone,
Of stone,
As they were made of stone.

Only Young Sampson
Made reply
As clear as Cornish gold,
For he and only he
Could tell
The salt song that she told,
She told,
The salt song that she told.

She beckoned where
Young Sampson stood.
He took her by the hand.
And one and one
They walked them down
Towards the Zennor strand,
The strand,
Towards the Zennor strand.

And did they ever
Come again
There's never a one
Will own,
Where still in church
The people stand
As they were made of stone,
Of stone,
As they were made of stone.

Zennor is on the coast of the far west of Cornwall, and is a village once renowned for its singers. The church, dedicated to the Virgin St Sinara or Sener, has a fifteenth-century bench-end bearing a splendid carving of its famous mermaid, complete with comb and glass.

How the Sea

'How the sea does shout,'
Says Danny Grout.
'Sounds very vexed.
What does it say?'
Feed me a wreck,
Said Sam-on-the-Shore.

'How the sea cries,'
Says Jimmy Wise.
'Early and late.
What does it say?'
Send me some freight,
Said Sam-on-the-Shore.

'How the sea moans,'
Said Johnnie Stones
Growing pale, then paler.
'What does it say?'
Send me a sailor,
Said Sam-on-the-Shore.

'Shall we sail today?'
Says Dan, says Jim,
Also John.
Don't fancy a cold swim.
Homeward we go, boys.
Put kettle on,
Said Sam-on-the-Shore.

Ramhead and Dodman

Said Ramhead to Dodman
  As proudly they stood
Their brows in the heavens
  Their feet in the flood,

'Of all the tall headlands
  That hold back the sea
Throughout Cornwall's kingdom,
  The greatest is me!'

Said Dodman to Ramhead,
  'Of all cliff-tops high
The stoutest, the strongest,
  The sturdiest am I!

'And never O never
  In cold or in heat
Old Ramhead and Dodman
  Together will meet.'

But softly the sea
  As they chanted their rhyme
Said, 'I'll swallow the pair of you
  All in good time.

'For deep in my belly
    There's room and to spare,
And I promise you both
    A safe meeting down there,

'Where mother nor father
    No sister nor brother
Will Ramhead and Dodman
    Tell one from the other,

'Though Dodman and Ramhead
    Today you may stand
Your heads in the heavens,
    Your feet in the sand.'

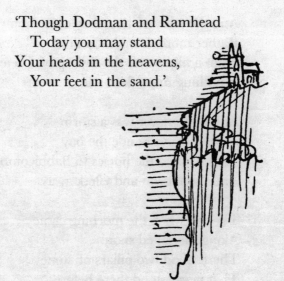

The Cornish saying 'When Ramhead and Dodman meet' means 'never'.
Rame Head (formerly known as Ramhead) and Dodman are headlands,
twenty-five miles apart, in south Cornwall.

The Parson and the Clerk

The Clerk stands in the ocean,
The Parson on the land,
From top to toe to fingertips
Red as the Devon sand.

The people of Teignmouth say
(And they say it at Shaldon, too)
That the Parson and the Clerk
Are sandstone through and through,

And the story of how they came home
Rather more drunk than dry
From a night with the Bishop of Exeter
Is nothing more than a lie.

And there never was a storm
As they drove beside the bay
That washed the horses to Babbicombe
And the Parson and Clerk away.

Though when the morning came
Along the salted shore
There stood two pillars of stone
That never stood there before.

And often, some folk say,
If you stand quite still and hark,
The Parson is taking a service
With responses from the Clerk.

But only the Parson and Clerk
Know the truth of the tale
And gently both of them wink an eye
As they stand on the sand and shale.

Says the Parson to the Clerk,
'Perhaps it is just as well
For the sake of their peace of mind
That they think we are stone and shell.

'And whether the day is bright
Or the night is wild and dark
Shall we let them believe it is so?'
'Amen,' says the Clerk.

This is a legend of Devonshire. If you have travelled by train along the coastline between Dawlish and Teignmouth, beyond Exeter, you will have passed the two rocks known as the Parson and the Clerk. 'Clerk' was the name given to a specially appointed layman whose duties included helping the parson at baptisms and marriages, and who also led the responses made by the church congregation during prayers.

Prince Ivo

Prince Ivo by the castle stood
He built with his own hand.
He looked towards the wandering sea,
He looked towards the land.

Tall was the yellow tower where
Prince Ivo's flag was flown.
The moat was wide, the moat was deep,
The gate was all of stone.

'And none there is,' Prince Ivo said,
'Shall bring my castle low,
For I am Lord of all I see
Wherever I may go.'

But there was one that heard him speak
And by his castle lay
Crept up the evening strand and washed
His house of sand away.

And when at sunfall Ivo came
Down to the silent shore
There was no sign of wall or tower.
His castle was no more.

Never a sign did Ivo show
Of sorrow or of pain,
But took his sturdy spade in hand
To build his house again.

Prince Ivo smiled and shook his head.
Softly I heard him say,
'Tomorrow, but tomorrow
Is another day.'

A Sailor Sat on the Watery Shore

A sailor sat on the watery shore
   By the side of the shiny sea,
And as the billows railed and roared
   These words he said to me.
'I've sailed to the Rock from Plymouth Dock
   And from Sydney to Simonstown,
And oh but it's true that a life on the blue
   Ain't the same as the life on the brown.

'For there's gusts and there's gales and there's spirting
     whales
   And there's fish flying round like a fountain,
And there's bays and there's bights and there's Great
     Northern Lights,
   And there's oceans as deep as a mountain.
And then there's your mates in the varying states
   From the angel and saint to the sinner,
Though I think you will find they are much of a kind
   When you sit down beside 'em for dinner.

'

'And yarns by the fathom you'll hear 'em all spin
   Of ghost-ships and sea-serpents mighty,
Of mermaids divine, and of Crossing the Line
   With King Neptune and Queen Amphitrite.
O many the lays I could sing of the days
   As in suits dazzling white from the dhoby[1]
We sauntered ashore in New York, Singapore,
   Or went up the line to Nairobi.

'And your eyes, my young friend, would jump out of
     your head,
   When the ship bade old England good-bye-ee,
At the antics of tars to the sound of guitars
   Whether strummed in Cadiz or Hawaii.
You may search the world through, but no friend is as
     true
   As the matelot so free and stout-hearted,
Though when he comes on leave (and to tell it, I
     grieve)
   There's no man from his pay sooner parted.

[1] the wash

'Furthermore,' said the sailor, 'it's certain to me
    As this beach is all covered with sand,
Though a sailor may find many sharks in the sea
    He will find even more on the land.'
'Ah, sailor,' I said, 'but I feel that your heart
    For the world of the wave is still yearning,
And I think I surmise from the look in your eyes
    That to it you'll soon be returning.'

'Good gracious!' the sailor said. 'Certainly not,
    And I can't think what gave you the notion
That once having left it, I'd wish to return
    To the dark, unpredictable ocean.
I've a nice little semi in Citadel Road
    That faces away from the sea,
And the reason it's thus – but, dear me, there's my bus
    And it's time for my afternoon tea!'

Dreamt Last Night

Dreamt last night of young Jack Swallow
With his fiddle and his bow
Sailed with us in *Kingston Sapphire*
Oceans high and low.

Seas lurched up and seas lurched down,
Sky was strong with wind and rain,
Jack he shrugged and Jack he whistled
'Happy Days Are Here Again'.

When the wave was in the messdeck,
When no spuds were in the bin,
When we worked an eight-hour trick
And the bread had weevils in,

When the guns had smoked, and midnight
Burned as brightly as the noon,
Jack it was played 'Philadelphia',
'Haul the Bowline', 'Bold Dragoon'.

Never a word of you, Jack Swallow,
Since our fortune was as one
In cold seas quiet as glass,
Seas the colour of the sun.

Where do you walk today, Jack Swallow?
Is it beneath a stranger star?
Do you lie under the blue, the green,
And is it near or far?

Still I hear your voice, Jack Swallow,
Through the darkness of the day;
Still I hear the songs you sang
And your fiddle play.

A trick is the time a sailor spends on watch or duty. An eight-hour trick is also known as 'watch on watch', or 'watch on, stop on': that is, on continuous duty for eight hours before a 'relief' comes on watch to take your place.

The Young Man of Cury

I am the Young Man of Cury,
I lie on the lip of the sand,
I comb the blown sea with five fingers
To call my true-love to the land.

She gave me a comb made of coral,
She told me to comb the green tide
And she would rise out of the ocean
To lie on the strand by my side.

Her hair flowed about her like water,
Her gaze it was blue, it was bold,
And half of her body was silver
And half of her body was gold.

One day as I lay by the flood-tide
And drew the bright comb to and fro
The sea snatched it out of my fingers
And buried it in the dark flow.

She promised me that she would teach me
All the hours of waking, of sleep,
The mysteries of her salt country,
The runes and the tunes of the deep;

How spells may be broken, how sickness
Be cured with a word I might tell,
The thief be discovered, the future
Be plain as these pebbles, this shell.

My son and his son and his also,
She said, would be heir to such charm
And their lives and their loves hold in safety
For ever from evil and harm.

But never a song does she sing me,
Nor ever a word does she say
Since I carried her safe where the tide-mark
Is scored on the sands of the bay.

I am the Young Man of Cury,
I lie on the lip of the sand,
I comb the blown sea with five fingers
To call my true-love to the land.

Cury is a village near Lizard Point in Cornwall. Cornish legends tell of how
a fisherman from Cury rescued a stranded mermaid and returned her to
the sea. Robert Hunt has a version called 'The Old Man of Cury' in his
Popular Romances of the West of England (1881), set in Kynance Cove, also in
the Lizard Peninsula.

When George the Fifth Was a Midshipman

When George the Fifth was a Midshipman
(Before he wore the crown)
He bought himself an African Grey
Ashore in Port Said town.
   God Save the King! said Charlotte.

She was quite the prettiest parrot
The Prince had ever seen.
The dragoman said she was six months old.
The Prince was seventeen.
   Shipmates for ever! said Charlotte.

She perched on the Prince's shoulder
(So to speak) for the rest of his life.
They say he loved that parrot
Almost as much as a wife.
   What about it? said Charlotte.

In HMS *Bacchante*
Three years they sailed the blue.
She'd hawk and squawk like an old sea-dog
When His Highness wasn't in view.
          Where's the Captain? said Charlotte.

One day at Buckingham Palace
She heard the city bells ring
And all the people of London
Cry out, 'God Save the King!'
          Me too, said Charlotte.

She sat at the right-hand corner
Of King George's royal throne.
There wasn't a single State Paper
She didn't know for her own.
          Mum's the word! said Charlotte.

When the King was ill and ailing
And very nearly died
They shut her out of the bedroom;
Left her in the passage outside.
                    Bless my buttons! said Charlotte.

But when his illness was ended
She was first at His Majesty's bed;
Danced for joy on the pillow
And over his anointed head.
                    God Saved the King! said Charlotte.

King George V (1865–1936) entered the Royal Navy when he was twelve, and acquired Charlotte, his pet parrot (an African Grey), when his ship called at Port Said. She was his great friend for most of his life. Charlotte had a loud, commanding voice like an old-fashioned sea-captain. Most (but not all) of the remarks she makes in the poem are phrases we are told she had picked up or had been taught to say.

Sailors

Spider Webb,
Blanco White,
Pincher Martin,
Shiner Bright,

Doughy Baker,
Dolly Gray,
Smudger Smith,
Piggy May,

Tottie Bell,
Bunny Lake,
Stole a peck
Of Navy cake.[1]

Soapy Watson,
Dodger Green,
Pedlar Palmer,
Daisy Dean,

Snip Taylor,
Charley Peace,
Moggie Morgan,
Bodger Lees,

Dusty Miller,
Twisty Lane,
Made them bring it
Back again.

[1] rather heavy slab cake on sale in naval canteens

Mrs Colón

Mrs Colón,
Christopher's gone
Sailing a boat
On the herring pond.

Says he's sure
That he knows best,
Steering, speering
West and west.

We gave him a call,
We gave him a shout
But he simply refuses
To turn about.

Will he remember
To keep in his head
The sooth of what
The schoolmaster said,

That the world is flat
With never a bend,
Go too far
And you're off the end?

Mrs Colón,
What's to be done?
Christopher's sailing
The herring pond.

In English-speaking countries the Italian sailor Cristoforo Colombo (or, in
Spain, Cristobal Colón) is known as Christopher Columbus.

Francesco de la Vega

Francesco de la Vega
From the hours of childhood
Passed his days
In the salt of the ocean.

Only one word he spoke.
Lierjanes! – the name
Of the sea-village of his birth
In the Year of God 1657.

While other children
Helped in field or kitchen,
Wandered the mountain-slope,
He swam the wild bay.

While others were at church
He dived to where lobster and squid
Lodged in the sea's dark cellar.
He must suffer a salt death, said Father Ramiro.

His mother and father entreated him
To come to his own bed.
His brothers and sisters called him
Home from the yellow sand-bar.

Amazed, they watched him
Arrow the waves like a young dolphin.
Until they tired of waiting, he hid
Under the mountain of black water.

On a night mad with storm
The waves rose high as the church-tower
And beat the shore like a drum.
He did not return with the morning.

Foolish boy, now he is drowned, they said.
His family added their salt tears to the ocean
As they cast on flowers and prayers.
In my opinion, he asked for it, said Father Ramiro.

Years flowed by: ten, twenty.
The village of Lierjanes forgot him.
Then, miles off Cadiz, herring fishermen
Sighted, at dawning, a sea-creature.

Three days they pursued him
Through the autumn waters;
Trapped him at last in strong nets
And brought him to land.

They gazed at his silver body in wonder;
At his pale eyes, staring always ahead;
At his hair, tight, and as a red moss.
What seemed like bright scales adorned his spine.

Most marvellous of all, instead
Of nails upon his feet and hands
There grew strange shells
That glowed gently like jewels of the sea.

When they questioned him
All he would reply was, *Lierjanes!*
Wrapping him in a soft white sailcloth
They laid him on a bed of linen.

A monk of Cadiz heard their story.
It is Francesco de la Vega,
The fish-boy of Lierjanes, he declared.
I shall bring him to his home and family.

Ah, but how his parents, brothers, sisters
Wept with happiness and welcomed him
With loving kisses and embraces, as though
Like Lazarus he had risen, and from a sea-grave!

But the young man returned no sign
Of love or recognition.
He gazed at them as though sightless;
Was indifferent to their sighs, their fondlings.

Long years he dwelt among them,
Never speaking, eating little,
Shifting unhappily in the decent clothes
With which they arrayed him.

One morning, nine years on,
He vanished from the house and hearth-side;
Was seen no more in the village of Lierjanes.
Great was the sadness of those who loved him!

Months, years ahead, two fishermen
Hauling across the stubborn waters
Of the Bay of Asturias
Sighted a sudden sea-creature at play.

Swiftly, and with spear and net,
They followed, but he escaped them.
As he rushed through the waves they heard a cry.
Lierjanes! Lierjanes!

Teignmouth

Teignmouth. Ox-red
Sand and scree.
The pier's long finger
Testing the sea.

Salt-damp deck-chairs
Along the Den.
Pierrots singing,
Here we are again!

Sand-artist crimping
The crocodile:
Quartz for a yellow eye,
Shells for a smile.

Punch kills the Baby.
The Mission sings a hymn.
Through the level water
The sailboats swim.

My father, slick
From his boots to his cap,
Driving the Doctor's
Pony and trap.

Here's my mother,
Lives next door,
Strolling with a sunshade
The long blue shore.

The sun and the day
Burn gold, burn green.
August Bank Holiday,
1914.

In with the evening
The tide runs grey;
Washes a world
Away, away.

A Day in Early Summer

A day in early summer
The first year of the war,
Davy Jones and I sat down
By the North Sea-shore.

The sun was bright, warm was the sand,
The sky was hot and blue.
How long we sat there
I never knew:

Rigged in brand-new uniforms,
Two naval sprogs
Dozing in the dancing sun,
Tired as dogs.

Suddenly a child's voice spoke
Across the silent shore:
'Look at those two sailors!
I wonder who they are?'

I sat up and looked about
The yellow and the blue
For the sailors on the shore.
I wondered, too.

Not a seaman could I see
As far as sight could reach:
Only the locked-up pier, the rolls
Of barbed-wire on the beach;

Only the tank-traps on the prom
By the shallow bay;
A woman and a little child
Wandering away;

Only Davy Jones and I
Wearing tiddley suits,
Lanyards, caps with 'HMS',
Shiny pussers'[1] boots.

God help England, then I thought,
Gazing out to sea,
If all between it and the foe
Is Davy Jones, and me.

[1] naval issue

Nursery Rhyme of Innocence
and Experience

I had a silver penny
   And an apricot tree
And I said to the sailor
   On the white quay

'Sailor O sailor
   Will you bring me
If I give you my penny
   And my apricot tree

'A fez from Algeria
   An Arab drum to beat
A little gilt sword
   And a parakeet?'

And he smiled and he kissed me
   As strong as death
And I saw his red tongue
   And I felt his sweet breath

'You may keep your penny
*   And your apricot tree*
And I'll bring your presents
*   Back from sea.'*

O the ship dipped down
    On the rim of the sky
And I waited while three
    Long summers went by

Then one steel morning
    On the white quay
I saw a grey ship
    Come in from sea

Slowly she came
    Across the bay
For her flashing rigging
    Was shot away

All round her wake
    The seabirds cried
And flew in and out
    Of the hole in her side

Slowly she came
    In the path of the sun
And I heard the sound
    Of a distant gun

And a stranger came running
    Up to me
From the deck of the ship
    And he said, said he

'O are you the boy
    Who would wait on the quay
With the silver penny
    And the apricot tree?

'I've a plum-coloured fez
    And a drum for thee
And a sword and a parakeet
    From over the sea.'

'O where is the sailor
    With bold red hair?
And what is that volley
    On the bright air?

'O where are the other
    Girls and boys?
And why have you brought me
    Children's toys?'

Outsiders and Insiders

Mr Pennycomequick

Mr Hector Pennycomequick
  Stood on the castle keep,
Opened up a carriage-umbrella
  And took a mighty leap.

'Hooray!' cried Mr Pennycomequick
  As he went through the air.
'I've always wanted to go like this
  From here to Newport Square.'

But Mr Hector Pennycomequick
  He never did float nor fly.
He landed in an ivy-bush,
  His legs up in the sky.

Mr Hector Pennycomequick
  They hurried home to bed
With a bump the size of a sea-gull's egg
  On the top of his head.

'So sorry,' said Mr Pennycomequick,
  'For causing all this fuss.
When next I go to Newport Square
  I think I'll take the bus.'

The moral of this little tale
  Is difficult to refute:
A carriage-umbrella's a carriage-umbrella
  And not a parachute.

Janny Jim Jan

Janny Jim Jan
The Cornish man
Walked out on Bodmin Moor,
A twist of rye
For a collar and tie
And his boots on backsyvore.[1]

'Janny Jim Jan,'
The children sang,
'Here's a letter from the King of Spain.'
But Janny turned nasty,
Hit 'em with a pasty,
Sent 'em home again.

[1] the wrong way round

Mrs McPhee

Mrs McPhee
Who lived in South Zeal
Roasted a duckling
For every meal.

'Duckling for breakfast
And dinner and tea,
And duckling for supper,'
Said Mrs McPhee.

'It's sweeter than sugar,
It's clean as a nut,
'I'm sure and I'm certain
It's good for me – but

'I don't like these feathers
That grow on my back,
And my silly webbed feet
And my voice that goes quack.'

As easy and soft
As a ship to the sea,
As a duck to the water
Went Mrs McPhee.

'I think I'll go swim
In the river,' said she;
Said Mrs Mac, Mrs Quack,
Mrs McPhee.

Brigid

Brigid, bring the cows
From the water shore
Now the sun is falling
Underneath the moor.

Bring them by the field-oak,
Bring them by the stone
That stands at the cross-way
With Bible pictures on.

In her hand she carries
A wand of green bay
As she brings the swaying herd
Slowly on its way.

The wild duck from their swimming,
The wild duck as they fly
Come at her calling
As she passes by.

Brigid, bring the cows
From the long shore
Bring the milk and butter
To the hungry poor.

St Brigid of Ireland is said to have founded the first nunnery in that country in about the sixth century. This was at Cill-Dara (the Church of the Oak), also now known as Kildare. Many legends and stories are told of her compassion, one of which is that as a farm-child she was sent by her parents to milk the cows, but gave away all the milk to the poor.

I Love My Darling Tractor

I love my darling tractor,
I love its merry din,
Its muscles made of iron and steel,
Its red and yellow skin.

I love to watch its wheels go round
However hard the day,
And from its bed inside the shed
It never thinks to stray.

It saves my arm, it saves my leg,
It saves my back from toil,
And it's merry as a skink when I give it a drink
Of water and diesel oil.

I love my darling tractor
As you can clearly see,
And so, the jolly farmer said,
Would you if you were me.

Maggie Dooley

Old Maggie Dooley
Twice a day
Comes to the Park
To search for the stray,
Milk in a bowl,
Scraps on a tray,
'Breakfast time!' 'Supper time!'
Hear her say.

Alone on a bench
She'll sit and wait
Till out of the bushes
They hesitate:
Tommy No-Tail
And Sammy No-Fur,
Half-Eye Sally
And Emmy No-Purr.

She sits by the children's
Roundabout
And takes a sip
From a bottle of stout.
She smiles a smile
And nods her head
Until her little
Family's fed.

Whatever the weather,
Shine or rain,
She comes at eight
And eight again.
'It's a Saint you are,'
To Maggie I said,
But she smiled a smile
And shook her head.

'Tom and Sammy,
Sally and Em,
They need me
And I need them.
I need them
And they need me.
That's all there is,'
She said, said she.

Riley

Down in the water-meadows Riley
Spread his wash on the bramble-thorn,
Sat, one foot in the moving water,
Bare as the day that he was born.

Candid was his curling whisker,
Brown his body as an old tree-limb,
Blue his eye as the jay above him
Watching him watch the minjies[1] swim.

Four stout sticks for walls had Riley,
His roof was a rusty piece of tin,
As snug in the lew[2] of a Cornish hedgerow
He watched the seasons out and in.

He paid no rates, he paid no taxes,
His lamp was the moon hung in the tree.
Though many an ache and pain had Riley
He envied neither you nor me.

Many a friend from bush or burrow
To Riley's hand would run or fly,
And soft he'd sing and sweet he'd whistle
Whatever the weather in the sky.

[1] small minnows
[2] lee

Till one winter's morning Riley
From the meadow vanished clean.
Gone was the rusty tin, the timber,
As if old Riley had never been.

What strange secret had old Riley?
Where did he come from? Where did he go?
Why was his heart as light as summer?
'Never know now,' said the jay. 'Never know.'

Little Lizzie Ivory

Little Lizzie Ivory
Who lives at Uffcombe View
Plays on the grand piano
At the early age of two.

She climbs upon the music stool
With zing and also zest
And spreads out all her pieces
Along the music rest.

She flexes every finger
And then she bends a wrist
In the most distinctive manner
Of the concert pianist.

Her hands fly up, her hands fly down
Just like a music star
In items of all kinds from her
Extensive repertoire.

She plays a guide to Italy,
She plays a guide to Spain
And a table giving times of every
Inter-City train.

She plays the morning paper,
The evening one as well
And a list of wines and spirits
From the landlord of *The Bell*.

She plays a sheet of foolscap
That is absolutely blank
And a paper full of figures
From the Trustee Savings Bank.

She plays the Christmas Catalogue
From Tamplin's Toy Bazaar
And volume one of quite a large
Encyclopaedia.

She plays the birthday letter
She had from Uncle Ned
And the telephone directory
From A right through to Z.

So if Miss Lizzie Ivory
Decides that she must call
To see the shining Steinway
That's just inside the hall,

Be sure that you have handy
On that very special day
The special sort of music
Miss Lizzie likes to play.

Don't Wake Up Lord Hazey

Don't wake up Lord Hazey,
Let him take his rest.
Let him snore – I'm certain sure
It's really for the best.

Don't wake up Lord Hazey,
Don't bother him at all.
I don't think he'd appreciate
An early-morning call.

Don't wake up Lord Hazey,
Let him dream and doze.
Don't take up a tea and toast
And don't lay out his clothes.

Don't wake up Lord Hazey,
I wouldn't think it wise
However shines the midday sun,
However blue the skies.

Don't wake up Lord Hazey,
Don't give him a shake.
There's just no knowing what he'll do
When he's wide awake.

Don't wake up Lord Hazey,
Don't give his door a knock
Whoever's on the telephone
Or what it is o'clock.

Don't wake up Lord Hazey,
And don't get in a fizz;
Better to leave Lord Hazey
Exactly where he is.

Mrs Bessie Busybody

Mrs Bessie Busybody,
I declare,
Knows all the news
And some to spare.

From six in the morning
On the dot
Peers through the window
To see what's what.

Who's up early?
Who's up late?
Who wrote that
On the schoolyard gate?

Who's getting better?
Who's getting worse?
Who's had a visit
From the District Nurse?

Who turned the dustbins
Upside down?
Who had a call
From P.C. Brown?

Who wasn't home
Till twelve last night?
Who broke his nose
In a fisticuff fight?

Who cracked the glass
In the garden frame?
Who didn't answer
When the rent-man came?

Who climbed the wall
At Number Five,
Took all the honey
Out of the hive,

Then as cool
As cool could be
Stole every apple
From the orchard tree?

Who let the bulldog
Off his chain?
Who had a case
Of best champagne?

Who's gone missing,
And who is due
To have a little baby
In a month or two?

Winter, spring-time,
Summer-time, fall,
Mrs Bessie Busybody
Knows it all.

King Foo Foo

King Foo Foo sat upon his throne
Dressed in his royal closes,
While all around his courtiers stood
With clothes-pegs on their noses.

'This action strange,' King Foo Foo said,
'My mind quite discomposes,
Though vulgar curiosity
A good king never shoses.'

But to the court it was as clear
As poetry or prose is:
King Foo Foo had not had a bath
Since goodness only knoses.

Till one fine day the Fire Brigade
Rehearsing with their hoses
(To Handel's 'Water Music' played
With many puffs and bloses)

Quite failed the water to control
In all its ebbs and floses
And simply drenched the King with sev-
Eral thousand gallon doses.

At this each wight (though impolite)
A mighty grin exposes.
'At last,' the King said, 'now I see
That all my court morose is!

'A debt to keep his courtiers glad
A monarch surely oweses,
And deep within my royal breast
A sporting heart reposes.'

So now each night its water bright
The Fire Brigade disposes
Over a King who smiles as sweet
As all the royal roses.

The Money Came in, Came in

My son Sam was a banjo man,
His brother played the spoons,
Willie Waley played the ukulele
And his sister sang the tunes:
        Sometimes sharp,
        Sometimes flat,
        It blew the top
        Off your Sunday hat,
        But no one bothered
        At a thing like that,
        And the money came in, came in.

Gussie Green played a tambourine,
His wife played the mandolin,
Tommy Liddell played a one-string fiddle
He made from a biscuit tin.
        Sometimes flat,
        Sometimes sharp,
        The noise was enough
        To break your heart,
        But nobody thought
        To cavil or carp,
        And the money came in, came in.

Clicketty Jones she played the bones,
Her husband the kettle-drum,
Timothy Tout blew the inside out
Of a brass euphonium.

       Sometimes sharp,
       Sometimes flat,
       It sounded like somebody
       Killing the cat,
       But no one bothered
       At a thing like that,
       And the money came in, came in.

Samuel Shute he played the flute,
His sister played the fife.
The Reverend Moon played a double bassoon
With the help of his lady wife.

       Sometimes flat,
       Sometimes sharp
       As a pancake
       Or an apple tart,
       But everyone, everyone
       Played a part
       And the money came in, came in

Diggory Prance

Diggory Prance, Diggory Prance
Paid his bills with a bit of a dance.

He took a whistle, he took a drum,
He'd trip it and skip it till kingdom come.

He danced for the butcher who brought him meat
The whole of the length of Shambles Street.

He danced for the baker who baked his bread.
He danced for the tailor, his needle and thread.

He danced for his rent, he danced for his rates.
He danced for the builder who fixed his slates.

He danced for the cobbler who mended his shoe,
He danced for the plumber, the painter too.

He danced for his light, he danced for his heat.
He danced for his takeaway, sour-and-sweet.

He danced for the dentist, the doctor, the draper.
He danced for the price of his daily paper –

Till came a day when, 'Now, dear Diggory, please,
It's time,' said the Mayor, 'for this nonsense to cease.

'You must settle in cash and in coin what you owe
Or I fear I must ask you to pack up and go.'

But all of the people cried, 'What? What? What?
    What?
Send away Diggory? Certainly not!

'Send away Diggory? Never a chance!
We *like* to see Diggory doing a dance!

'We trust we are making it perfectly plain –
So please never mention the subject again.

'Never, whatever the wind or the weather,
Please never mention the subject again

'Of Diggory Prance, Diggory Prance
Who pays his bills with a bit of a dance.'

King Ezra

King Ezra was a drover
Walked the grey miles to town,
His sceptre was a hazel stick,
A billycock his crown.

His head was whiter than the frost,
His beard white as the floe;
He stood as strong as a stone man
Of Michelangelo.

A sack about his shoulders
In summer and in snow,
And on each foot an army boot
Was splintered at the toe.

Gently he drove the cattle
And softly led the sheep
As he went up to market
Under the Castle Keep.

And if the flock was hasty
Or herd was slow to hand,
He spoke the secret language
All creatures understand.

And never a one would wander
And never a one would stray
As he passed by our window
On Cattle Market Day.

I never heard him call nor cry
Nor saw him strike a blow,
Though in his hand the hazel wand
Was stern as iron crow.

Of all the men to come my way
In days of storm, of calm,
King Ezra wears for me the crown,
King Ezra bears the palm.

I see him as I saw him then
Seasons and worlds ago:
The Good King Ezra whose true name
I never was to know.

There Was an Old Woman

There was an old woman of Chester-le-Street
Who chased a policeman all over his beat.

She shattered his helmet and tattered his clothes
And knocked his new spectacles clean off his nose.

'I'm afraid,' said the Judge, 'I must make it quite clear
You can't get away with that sort of thing here.'

'I can and I will,' the old woman she said,
'And I don't give a fig for your water and bread.

'I don't give a hoot for your cold prison cell,
And your bolts and your bars and your handcuffs as
    well.

'I've never been one to do just as I'm bid.
You can put me in jail for a year!'

                                        So they did.

Said the Clown

Said the clown in the seven-ring circus
As he dived in a bucket of sand,
'Why nobody claps at my quips and my cracks
Is something I can't understand.

'The start of my act's a selection
Of millions and millions of jokes,
Then like wind and like fire I whizz down a wire
On a bike with one wheel and no spokes.

'When I fill up my pockets with water
And paint my face red, white and blue,
Folk stare at the ground and they don't make a sound.
I can't think of the reason. Can you?'

My Friend Mr Rory O'Donnell

My friend Mr Rory O'Donnell
Who lives in a house next the sea
Each morning at ten
Retires to his den
And sits silent from breakfast to tea.
And neither a word does he utter
Nor ever a note does he sigh,
But fixes his gaze
In a kind of a daze
On the ocean or maybe the sky.

And sometimes he taps with his fingers
Or waves them about in the air,
But most of the day
He's contented to stay
Quite perfectly still in his chair.
And now and again as he listens
A look in his eye makes it clear
That he's suddenly found
A strain or a sound
That nobody else seems to hear.

Then he calls out for pencil and paper
And rulers and pens by the score
And he struggles and strives
Drawing lines (all in fives)
And sprinkles them over galore
With sketches of hooks and of hangers
And things like an egg in a shell,
And dashes and dots
And little black blots
And words in *Italian* as well.

There's nobody here is quite certain
What Rory O'Donnell is at,
And the neighbours all say
He sends them away
When they knock on his door for a chat.
Perhaps we should send for a Doctor
Or a Priest or a Vicar should call,
Or maybe a few
Men in Very Dark Blue?
We can't think what he's up to at all.

Sal Scratch

Sal Scratch
Wore her husband's cap
The dust and the dirt to beat,
An apron of sack
And one on her back
And wellingtons on her feet.

With bucket and mop
She'd hardly stop
For a cup of strong tea at eleven,
And in shine or slush
Her steps she'd brush
Till they looked like the path to heaven.

With verve and vim
Both out and in
For her home she'd lovingly care
From the front-door brass
To the panes of glass
In the skylight over the stair.

She'd have been quite a Turk
If when home from his work
Her husband came in through the door
Without putting his feet
On each newspaper sheet
Laid out on the kitchen floor.

You may think such a house
Over-clean for her spouse,
But there neither was sorrow nor strife,
For by dirt and by dust
He was equally fussed
And as good (or as bad) as his wife.

When a Cornishwoman puts on old clothes to do her housework in, she is
said to look like 'Sal Scratch'.

Here's the Reverend Rundle

Here's the Reverend Rundle
His gear in a bundle,
He has a dog
He has a sled
And thousands of stories
In his head
And coloured pictures
Of the Holy Scriptures
To show, show
The Indians red
Who had picture and story
And saints in glory
And a heavenly throne
Of their very own
But were so well-bred
That they met him like a brother
And they loved each other
It was said,
The Reverend Rundle
And the Indians red
And through the Rockies
They watched him go
Over the ice
And under the snow –
But this was a very long
Time ago,
A long, long, long, long
Time ago.

They loved him from
His heels to his hat
As he rode on the rough
Or walked on the flat
Whether he stood
Or whether he sat,
The Reverend Rundle
His gear in a bundle
And as well as that
His favourite cat
Warm in a poke
Of his sealskin cloak
For fear some son
Of a hungry gun
Ate her for supper
In Edmonton
And they loved each other
It was said,
The Reverend Rundle
And the Indians red
And through the Rockies
They watched him go
Over the ice
And under the snow –
But this was a very long
Time ago,
A long, long, long, long
Time ago.

Tabitha Tupper

Tabitha Tupper
Had frogs for supper,
Joshua Jones had snails.
Fidelity Flutter
Had seaweed butter
(I think it comes from Wales).

Jeremy Croop
Had sting-nettle soup
Flavoured with gingerbread.
Dorothy Dart
Had fungus tart
With a kind of chocolate spread.

Timothy Lamb
Had jellyfish jam
Spread with Devonshire cream.
Christopher Hawke
Had bubble-and-squawk
(He said it tasted a dream).

Nathan Newell
Had winter gruel
That's made from curry and cheese.
William Wade
Had marmalade
Sprinkled with prunes and peas.

But sad to tell
They felt far from well
When they went up to bed,
And 'Why it's so
We just don't know!'
Their parents sighed and said,

While Tabitha Tupper
And all the others
Scarcely closed an eye,
And felt ever-so-slightly
Better-go-lightly,
And simply couldn't say why.

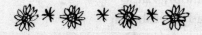

Mr Zukovsky

When Mr Augustus Zukovsky
First met his intended-to-be
His friends they all moaned and they grizzled and
  groaned,
'You just *can't* think of marrying she!
Why, she's clumsy, they say, as a camel
(If camels *are* clumsy, that is).
The mere thought of it, Mr Zukovsky,
Is fetching us all in a fizz!

'It looks as if what she is wearing
Was fired at her out of a gun,
And the state of her hair is her mother's despair
And like rays sticking out of the sun.
While as for you, Mr Zukovsky,
You're always so sober and neat,
And it's very well known how you brush and you comb
Before you set off down the street.

'She's a voice like the Seven Stones Lighthouse
When it's speaking of fogs or of gales,
And if she should whisper a secret
You can hear it from Windsor to Wales.
She's no ear whatever for music
And she can't tell a sharp from a flat.
When they're playing the National Anthem
She doesn't know what they are at.

'The money it slides through her fingers,
She can't sew, she can't clean, she can't cook,
And she spends half the day (so the neighbours all say)
With her nose in a *poetry* book.'
But to Mr Augustus Zukovsky
Such words were a slander and shame,
And he walked up the aisle with a beautiful smile
And he married his love just the same.

Now Mr and Mrs Zukovsky
For twenty-five years have been wed,
And there isn't a happier couple
In the whole of the kingdom, it's said.
They've a dog and two cats and five children,
A budgie, a buck and a doe,
And you won't find a jollier family
Though you search the world high and then low.

And as for those friends and companions
Who prophesied nothing but woe,
They all of them cry (without winking an eye),
'But we always *said* it would be so,
They're so awf'ly well suited, you know!
Yes, we always said it would be so,
We ALWAYS said it would be so, and so,
We *always* said it would be so.'

There Once Was a Man

There once was a man
Called Knocketty Ned
Who wore his cat
On top of his head.
Upstairs, downstairs,
The whole world knew
Wherever he went
The cat went too.

He wore it at work,
He wore it at play,
He wore it to town
On market-day,
And for fear it should rain
Or the snowflakes fly
He carried a brolly
To keep it dry.

He never did fret
Nor fume because
He always knew
Just where it was.
'And when,' said Ned,
'In my bed I lie
There's no better nightcap
Money can buy.'

'There's no better bonnet
To be found,'
Said Knocketty Ned,
'The world around.
And furthermore
Was there ever a hat
As scared a mouse
Or scared a rat?'

Did ever you hear
Of a tale like that
As Knocketty Ned's
And the tale of his cat?

John, John the Baptist

John, John the Baptist
Lived in a desert of stone,
He had no money,
Ate beans and honey,
And he lived quite on his own.

His coat was made of camel,
His belt was made of leather,
And deep in the gleam
Of a twisting stream
He'd stand in every weather.

John, John the Baptist
Worked without any pay,
But he'd hold your hand
And bring you to land
And wash your fears away.

Old Billy Ricky

Old Billy Ricky
Lives down a well
Snug as a silver
Snail in a shell,
Sits all day
On a mossy shelf
Keeping himself
(He says) to himself,
Whistles and watches
The circle of sky
As weathers and seasons
Pass him by.

Nothing to eat
But plenty to drink,
How can he ever
Sleep a wink,
Back pressed tight
To a ferny wall,
Nothing to catch him
If he should fall,
And what for mercy's
Sake can he see
In a newt and a frog
For company?

But there he sits
In his round stone room
The green moss glimmering
In the gloom,
And if you should ask
On the village square
How long Billy's
Been down there
There's nobody knows
Wherefore or why
And if you ask *him*
You won't get a reply:
He simply won't answer,
He never will tell
Won't old Billy Ricky.

Well! Well! Well!

Willoughby

Willoughby Whitebody-Barrington-Trew
Could never decide what the weather would do.
Out of his window he'd gaze by the hour
To see if it might be a shine or a shower.
He'd open the closet that's under the stair
And he'd hem and he'd haw as to what he should wear,
And often as not (and I'm stating a fact)
By the time he set off it was time to come back.

He'd wait by the hat-stand inside the front door
And ask himself hundreds of questions, or more.
'Will it snow? Will it blow? Will it rain? Will it hail?
Will these summery breezes turn into a gale?
Is the temperature likely to rise or to fall?
Do you think that we're in for a bit of a squall?
Although the sun's shining,' he'd say with a groan,
'It'll come down in buckets before I get home.'

'Shall I get me a waterproof? Put on a coat?
An ulster that buttons right up to my throat?
A bowler? A beret? A felt or a straw?
The finest glengarry that ever you saw?
Am I needing a panama hat or a cane?
A carriage-umbrella to keep off the rain?
Is it Wellington weather or sandal or shoe?
I'm ashamed to confess that I haven't a clue.
There's no doubt about it,' said Willoughby White,
'Whatever I do I just can't get it right –
And if folk say I'm crazy I don't care a jot,
So I might as well go out dressed up in the lot.'

And every item in closet and hall
He took until nothing was left there at all.
'You may sneer,' declared Willoughby, 'or you may
   scoff,
But if it's too hot you can take something off.'
And he'd say to himself till his breath was all gone,
'If you haven't it with you, you can't put it on.'
Said Willoughby Whitebody-Barrington who
Could never decide what the weather would do.

Jack the Treacle Eater

Here comes Jack the Treacle Eater,
Never swifter, never sweeter,
With a peck of messages,
Some long, some shorter,
From my Lord and Master's quarter
(Built like a minaret)
Somewhere in Somerset.
> *Jack, how do you make such speed*
> *From banks of Tone to banks of Tweed*
> *And all the way back?*
> 'I train on treacle,' says Jack.

Here's one for Sam Snoddy
(Cantankerous old body).
'Will you come for Christmas dinner
With Missus and Squire?'
'Not on your life,' says Sam.
'Rather eat bread and jam
By my own fire.'

      Jack, how do you trot so spry
      The long road to Rye
      Bearing that heavy pack?
      'I train on treacle,' says Jack.

Here's one for Sally Bent
Lives in a gypsy tent
Down at Land's End.
'Will you sing at my daughter's bridal?'
'No,' says Sally. 'I'm too idle.
Besides, I've not much choice
Since up to Bodmin I lost my voice.'

      Jack, how do you travel so light
      From morning star through half the night
      With never a snack?
      'I train on treacle,' says Jack.

Here's one for Trooper Slaughter,
Retired, of Petherwin Water.
'Dear Tom, will you come
And we'll talk of our days with the drum,
Bugle, fife and the cannon's thunder.'
'Too late,' says Tom, 'old chum.
I'm already six feet under.'

> *Jack, how do you care for your wife*
> *If you run all the days of your life?*
> *Is it something the rest of us lack?*
> 'I train on treacle,' says Jack.

The original Jack lived in Somerset and was a famous runner who took messages to and from London for the Messiter family of Barwick Park, near Yeovil. He is said to have trained on treacle, and is commemorated there by one of four follies (useless but usually delightful and expensive buildings put up for fun) built by George Messiter in the early nineteenth century. On top of Jack's Folly is a figure of Hermes (representing Jack), the Greek messenger and herald of the gods. At midnight, Jack is said to climb down from his folly and go to the lake by the great house in order to quench his tremendous thirst caused by eating so much treacle.

Send for Solomon Fingergreen

Send for Solomon Fingergreen
As fast as you can go
For nothing in the garden
Is looking like to grow.
When I got up at dawning
The sun was rising bright
But everything in the garden
It looked a sorry sight.
When I looked out at noonday
The morning sun had shone
But everything in the garden
Was looking wisht[1] and wan.

Send for Solomon Fingergreen,
Ring his front door bell,
Tell him that the garden
Is looking far from well.
Ask him to bring his barrow,
His fork and spade and hoe,
And what's to nip and what's to snip
He's very sure to know.
Ask him to bring his dibble,
His mattock and his bill,
For it seems to me the garden
Is looking rather ill.

[1] unwell or sad

Send for Solomon Fingergreen,
Fetch him at the run,
For only Solomon Fingergreen
Will know what's to be done,
For Solomon has the country tongue,
And silent he will say,
And all green things will listen
And all green things obey,
Though where he learned the speaking
And how he earned the spell
Is something Solomon Fingergreen
Will never ever tell.

You may think to give him silver
But this he won't allow.
He says it's a gift of the gods, you see,
He got he don't know how.
But if the green of the garden
Is looking far from spry,
'Send for Solomon Fingergreen,'
Is what the neighbours cry.
'Send for Solomon Fingergreen
Who year by turning year
Speaks the deep green speeches
That everything green will hear.'

Annabel-Emily

Annabel-Emily Huntington-Horne
Who lives at Threepenny Cam
From the very first moment that she was born
Would eat nothing whatever but jam.

They offered her milk, they offered her bread,
They offered her biscuits and beans
But Annabel-Emily shook her head
And made the most horrible scenes.

They offered her chicken, and also a choice
Of sausage or cheese or Spam[1]
But Annabel screamed at the top of her voice,
'Can't you see what I'm wanting is JAM?'

Her parents they wept like the watery bay
And they uttered and spluttered such cries
As, 'She's perfectly certain to waste away
In front of our very own eyes!'

[1] proprietary name for a particular brand of tinned, spiced ham loaf which
first became well known in Britain during the Second World War.

But Annabel-Emily Huntington-Horne,
Her hair the colour of snow,
Still lives in the cottage where she was born
A hundred years ago.

Her tooth is as sugary sweet today
As ever it was before
And as for her hundred years, they say
She's good for a hundred more.

She's pots of apricot, strawberry, peach
In twos and threes and fours
On yards and yards of shelves that reach
From the ceilings to the floors.

She's jars of currants red and black
On every chest and chair
And plum and gooseberry in a stack
On every step of the stair.

Raspberry, cranberry, blackberry, or
Apple, damson, quince –
There never was better jam before
Nor will ever be better since.

For Annabel of Threepenny Cam,
Whose ways are quite well known,
Has never been one for boughten[2] jam
And always makes her own.

But if, when you are passing by,
She invites you for tea and a treat
Be careful just how you reply
If your taste and tooth aren't sweet:

Or it's certain (all the neighbours warn)
You'll be in a terrible jam
With Annabel-Emily Huntington-Horne
Who lives at Threepenny Cam.

---

[2] dialect word meaning something bought in a shop as opposed to being home-made.

My Neighbour Mr Normanton

My neighbour Mr Normanton
Who lives at ninety-five
'S as typical an Englishman
As any one alive.

He wears pin-stripes and bowler-hat.
His accent is sublime.
He keeps a British bull-dog
And British Summer Time.

His shoes are always glassy black
(He never wears the brown);
His brolly's rolled slim as a stick
When he goes up to town.

He much prefers a game of darts
To mah-jong or to chess.
He fancies Chelsea for the Cup
And dotes on G. & S.

Roast beef and Yorkshire pudding are
What he most likes to eat.
His drinks are tea and British beer
And sometimes whisky (neat).

And in his British garden
Upon St George's Day
He hoists a British Union Jack
And shouts, 'Hip, hip, hooray!'

But tell me, Mr Normanton,
That evening after dark,
Who were those foreign gentlemen
You met in Churchill Park?

You spoke a funny language
I couldn't understand;
And wasn't that some microfilm
You'd hidden in your hand?

And then that note I saw you post
Inside a hollow tree!
When I jumped out you turned about
As quick as quick could be.

Why did you use a hearing-aid
While strolling in the park
And talking to that worried-looking
Admiralty clerk?

The day you took the cypher-book
From underneath a stone,
I'm certain, Mr Normanton,
You thought you were alone.

Your powerful transmitter!
The stations that you call!
I love to watch you through the crack
That's in my bedroom wall.

Oh, thank you, Mr Normanton,
For asking me to tea.
It's really all quite riveting
To clever chaps like me.

What? Will I come and work for you?
Now please don't mention pay.
What super luck I left a note
To say I'd run away!

Is that a gun that's in your hand?
And look! A lethal pill!
And that's a real commando-knife?
I say, this is a thrill!

Of course I've never said a word
About the things you do.
Let's keep it all a secret
Between just me and . . .

Daniel Gumb

Daniel Gumb lived all alone
In a Cornish cave of granite stone,
Granite table and chair and bed,
Granite pillow to rest his head,
Granite roof and granite floor
And a sliding, gliding granite door
By Cheesewring Hill on Bodmin Moor.

He studied the stars and planets and then
(Hammer and chisel for a pen)
He chipped the drift of what he'd found
On bits of rock that lay around,
And over the moor the folk would come
For there wasn't a problem, wasn't a sum
As couldn't be solved by Daniel Gumb.

Daniel Gumb in the midst of life
Took to himself a loving wife.
She shared his crowst,[1] she shared his cell,
She gave him a gaggle of Gumbs as well
And he wrote on a stone for all to see:
'1735. D.G.'

Stranger, under Cheesewring Hill
In summer sun, in winter chill,
Search for the stone. It lies there still.

---

[1] food

Famous in his day, the stone-cutter Daniel Gumb was known as 'The Mountain Philosopher'. He died in 1776 and is buried in the parish of Linkinhorne.

Sir Frederick

Stiffly Sir Frederick
Stumps the green cobble-stones,
Opens the gate
By the stable door,
Hums as he strolls
In the pale of the afternoon
A faded old song
Of the First World War.

He lifts up his feet
Like a stork by the river bed,
Treads the long grass
Where the narcissi lean,
Plucks perhaps six or seven,
And at a sting-nettle
Strikes with his infantry-
Officer's cane.

Then in the library
Of his great mansion,
Books at attention
On every shelf,
Shakily signs his name
In his biography,
Serves tea and Dundee cake,
Has some himself.

Just as I drive away
I catch a glimpse of him
Dodging as best he can
Bullets of rain,
And as a thunder-clap
Bursts like a howitzer
He melts in the history
Books once again.

Sawson Sly

Sawson Sly
Open your eye,
Here's a maid says
You married her
Last July,
Promised a cottage
Of slate and stone
Your grannie had given you
For your own,
An orchard of seven
Apple trees,
A lop-eared pig
And a hive of bees,
Five milch cows,
A field of hay
And a pony and trap
For market day;
Swears the Parson
Made you a pair
Twelve of the clock
At Calstock Fair.

She's come with her daddy,
She's come with her mam
And a dear little darling
In a pram,
And just beyond
The garden gate
Her ten tall brothers
Stand and wait.
She's a shiny ring
As once was yours
And says you turned her
Out of doors
With never a coat,
A bonnet or cap.
Sawson, what do you say
To that?

Sawson Sly
Open your eye,
Here's a maid says
You married her
Last July.

Billy Medals

Do you know Billy Medals
That warrior bold,
His stars made of silver,
His circles of gold?
O there don't seem a battle
Of land, sea or air
For fifty years past
But old Bill wasn't there.

He stands on the corner
As straight as a gun,
And his circles and stars
Catch the rays of the sun.
His stars and his circles
All glitter and gleam,
And just like the rainbow
His ribbons they beam.

You must know Billy Medals
With his chestful of gongs,
He knows all the war-stories
And all the war-songs.
His jacket is ragged,
His trousers are green,
And no one stands straighter
For 'God Save the Queen'.

Around his torn topper
Are badges in scores
Of goodness knows how many
Different corps.
But in war Billy Medals
Has never known harm
For he's never been farther
Than Fiveacre Farm.

When lads from the village
Dodged shrapnel and shell,
Billy Medals was cleaning out
Wishworthy Well.
When in deserts they sweated,
In oceans they froze,
Billy Medals was scaring
The rooks and the crows.

Did you see the brave soldier
New-home from the war
Give Billy the star
That once proudly he bore?
Billy Medals he cackled
And capered with glee
And the village-boys laughed,
But the soldier, not he.

Figgie Hobbin

Nightingales' tongues, your majesty?
    Quails in aspic, cost a purse of money?
Oysters from the deep, raving sea?
    Grapes and Greek honey?
Beads of black caviare from the Caspian?
    Rock melon with corn on the cob in?
Take it all away! grumbled the old King of Cornwall.
    Bring me some figgie hobbin!

Devilled lobster, your majesty?
    Scots kail brose or broth?
Grilled mackerel with gooseberry sauce?
    Cider ice that melts in your mouth?
Pears filled with nut and date salad?
    Christmas pudding with a tanner or a bob in?[1]
Take it all away! groused the old King of Cornwall.
    Bring me some figgie hobbin!

Amber jelly, your majesty?
    Passion fruit flummery?
Pineapple sherbet, milk punch or Pavlova cake,
    Sugary, summery?
Carpet-bag steak, blueberry grunt, cinnamon
        crescents?
    Spaghetti as fine as the thread on a bobbin?

---

[1] slang for sixpence (2½p) and a shilling (5p) in 'old' money

Take it all away! grizzled the old King of Cornwall.
  Bring me some figgie hobbin!

So in from the kitchen came figgie hobbin,
  Shining and speckled with raisins sweet,
And though on the King of Cornwall's land
  The rain it fell and the wind it beat,
As soon as a forkful of figgie hobbin
  Up to his lips he drew,
Over the palace a pure sun shone
  And the sky was blue.
THAT'S what I wanted! he smiled, his face
  Now as bright as the breast of the robin.
To cure the sickness of the heart, ah —
  Bring me some figgie hobbin!

Figgie hobbin is a Cornish pudding sweetened with raisins, which are
known as 'figs' in Cornwall. It may be eaten either with meat, or (with the
addition of more raisins) as a sweet.

Sam Groom

What are you writing down there, Sam Groom,
All alone in a deep, damp room,
Nose on the paper, tongue held tight,
What are you writing by candle-light?
   Words, says Sam.
   That's what I am.

Why do you write down there, Sam Groom,
While the bright bees buzz and the roses bloom?
Scribble and scrape goes your pen all day
As the sun and summer waste away.

Are you writing to your mammy or your daddy, Sam
     Groom,
Squinting your eye in the candle-fume,
To your brother or your sister or your own true-love
Or a friend or a foe that we know not of?

Is it a sermon or a bill of sale,
A shilling-shocker or a nursery-tale?
Is it blank, blank verse or a tally of rhymes
Or a letter to the Editor of *The Times?*

Are you putting the wrongs to rights, Sam Groom,
As you sit in a kitchen as chill as the tomb?
Is it songs for the owl or songs for the lark
Or a tune to whistle against the dark?

They say that you'll stay where you are, Sam Groom,
From half past nothing to the day of doom.
What are you writing down there, Sam Groom,
All alone in a deep, damp room?
  Words, says Sam.
  That's what I am.

Myth and Fable

Jill and Jack

Jill and Jack walked up the track
To find a pool of morning dew.
They took a pole, they took a pail,
Carried them both between the two.

Mani the Moon jumped low, jumped high,
Snatched them up into the sky.
Mani the Moon with fingers cold
Locked them in his house of gold.

When the moon is full and fair
You still may see them standing there,
And there they'll stay, I'm certain sure,
A thousand thousand years and more.

Pole and pail between the two:
Jill and Jack who walked the track
To find a pool of morning dew
And never came back. Poor Jill. Poor Jack.

Green Man in the Garden

Green man in the garden
    Staring from the tree,
Why do you look so long and hard
    Through the pane at me?

Your eyes are dark as holly,
    Of sycamore your horns,
Your bones are made of elder-branch,
    Your teeth are made of thorns.

Your hat is made of ivy-leaf,
    Of bark your dancing shoes,
And evergreen and green and green
    Your jacket and shirt and trews.

Leave your house and leave your land
    And throw away the key,
And never look behind, he creaked,
    And come and live with me.

I bolted up the window,
  I bolted up the door,
I drew the blind that I should find
  The green man never more.

But when I softly turned the stair
  As I went up to bed,
I saw the green man standing there.
  Sleep well, my friend, he said.

Colonel Fazackerley

Colonel Fazackerley Butterworth-Toast
Bought an old castle complete with a ghost,
But someone or other forgot to declare
To Colonel Fazack that the spectre was there.

On the very first evening, while waiting to dine,
The Colonel was taking a fine sherry wine,
When the ghost, with a furious flash and a flare,
Shot out of the chimney and shivered, 'Beware!'

Colonel Fazackerley put down his glass
And said, 'My dear fellow, that's really first class!
I just can't conceive how you do it at all.
I imagine you're going to a Fancy Dress Ball?'

At this, the dread ghost gave a withering cry.
Said the Colonel (his monocle firm in his eye),
'Now just how you do it I wish I could think.
Do sit down and tell me, and please have a drink.'

The ghost in his phosphorous cloak gave a roar
And floated about between ceiling and floor.
He walked through a wall and returned through a pane
And backed up the chimney and came down again.

Said the Colonel, 'With laughter I'm feeling quite
   weak!'
(As trickles of merriment ran down his cheek).
'My house-warming party I hope you won't spurn.
You *must* say you'll come and you'll give us a turn!'

Whereupon, the poor spectre – quite out of his wits –
Proceeded to shake himself almost to bits.
He rattled his chains and he clattered his bones
And he filled the whole castle with mumbles and moans.

But Colonel Fazackerley, just as before,
Was simply delighted and called out, 'Encore!'
At which the ghost vanished, his efforts in vain,
And never was seen at the castle again.

'Oh dear, what a pity!' said Colonel Fazack.
'I don't know his name, so I can't call him back.'
And then with a smile that was hard to define,
Colonel Fazackerley went in to dine.

The Old Lord of Trecrogo

Long, long ago-go
The old Lord of Trecrogo
Sat in his fougu
On a green granite boulder
Under Hawk's Tor,
Round his head a band of gold,
A red-legged crow
Standing on his shoulder
And at his feet
His Wise Men four.

'Who's that at the door?'
Said the Old Lord of Trecrogo.
'Someone's been waiting
For a month or more.
What do you think
I pay you for?
Is it friend or foe,
I want to know?
Why don't you rise up
And go, go, go?'

'Might be Mazey Jack,'
Said Siblyback,
'Come Christmassing, I fear,
Wrong time of year.'
'Might be All-Made-Of-Bone,'
Hummed Woolstone
Through his ivory comb.
'If you ask me, friend,
Best to pretend
No one's at home.'

'May be Tall Tide,'
Old Craddock cried,
'Sliding ashore
Under the front door.'
'All wrong,' said Witheybrook.
'I just had a look.
To my sorrow,
I think it's Tomorrow,
Nothing less, nothing more,
Scatting on the door.'

'*Tomorrow?* Oh! Oh!'
Said the old Lord of Trecrogo.
'Tomorrow that's knocking?
Tomorrow? That's shocking!
None can outpace him.
Who'll go and face him?
Can't someone deal him
A blow, like so? Or so?'
Said the old Lord of Trecrogo.

'Not me,' said Siblyback.
'Nor me,' said Woolstone.
'Not me,' said Old Craddock.
Said Witheybrook, 'Can't be done.'
'Can't believe what I've heard!'
The old Lord averred.
'Now I have only one true friend,
I wonder, I wonder whether—'
But, 'No go! No go! No go!'
Said the red-legged crow
And never budged a feather.
            And Tomorrow came on.

Eagle One, Eagle Two

Eagle one, eagle two,
Standing on the wall,
Your wings a-spread are made of lead,
You never fly at all.

High on the roof, Britannia
Holds her fishing-prong,
And she and they as white as clay
Stand still the whole day long.

And one looks to the eastward,
One to the setting sun,
And one looks down upon the town
Until the day is done.

But when the quarter-jacks their twelve
Upon the black town beat,
And when the moon's a gold balloon
Blowing down Castle Street,

Then with her spear, Britannia
The eagles both will guide
To drink their fill under the hill
Down by the riverside.

And when the Town Hall quarter-jacks
The hour of one beat plain,
Eagles and queen may all be seen
On wall and roof again.

But now I am a grown man
And hear the midnight bell,
Ask, is it true, the tale I knew
That still the children tell?

I only know at midnight
Softly I go by,
Nor look at all on roof and wall.
Do not ask me why.

In the Willow Gardens

In the Willow Gardens
Where once was wood and brake
A hundred town allotments
Come down to Harper's Lake.
In the Willow Gardens
Under the castle keep
A hundred town allotments
Stand beside the steep.

And here Tom tends his cabbage plants
And digs his taters out,
And leans upon a smudgy spade
To watch his Brussels sprout;
And brother Jack spreads chicken wire
For fear the fowls should stray,
And nails up bits of galvanized
To keep the wind away.

But in the Willow Gardens
I don't hear Tom nor Jack,
But I can hear the huntsmen
Along the forest track.
All through the Willow Gardens
I see them riding plain,
The iron knights of Normandy
And Robert of Mortain.

They ride along by Harper's Lake
Beside the water clear;
They hunt the hare, they hunt the boar,
They hunt the running deer.
Hark, I hear the hoof-beats,
I hear the hunters cry,
I hear them blow the hunting-horn,
I see the arrows fly!

'Don't you see them, Tommy,
And don't you see them, Jack?
And how they ride by the stream-side
To the wood's end and back?'
But Tommy shakes his silver head
And Jackie slaps his knee.
'There's nothing here,' says Jack to Tom.
'Maze[1] as a brush!' says he.

And Tommy goes on digging,
And Jackie bangs a nail.
'Better go home,' they say to me.
'You'm looking wisht[2] and pale.'
But still I see the huntsmen
Riding low and high
As plain as I see Jack and Tom.
I do not tell a lie.

[1] crazy
[2] unwell

Trim-and-Tall

Trim-and-Tall
Sat on the mountain,
Dabbled his feet
Where the waves ran in,
Tilted his bonnet,
Stretched his fine fingers
The compass round
For what he might win.

Trim-and-Tall
Speered down the valley,
The twisting river,
The hill, the plain;
Saw people striving,
Loving, living
In every season
Of shine, of rain.

Trim-and-Tall
Watched them raise up
Those who faltered, who fell
In the world's weather;
Saw them cheer
Those who wept,
Journeying always onward
Together, together.

Trim-and-Tall
On the mountain sat,
All he could wish
At his hand in fee.
I saw him there
Lonely and long,
And Trim-and-Tall sighed
Endlessly.

Miller's End

When we moved to Miller's End,
    Every afternoon at four
A thin shadow of a shade
    Quavered through the garden-door.

Dressed in black from top to toe
    And a veil about her head
To us all it seemed as though
    She came walking from the dead.

With a basket on her arm
    Through the hedge-gap she would pass,
Never a mark that we could spy
    On the flagstones or the grass.

When we told the garden-boy
    How we saw the phantom glide,
With a grin his face was bright
    As the pool he stood beside.

'That's no ghost-walk,' Billy said.
   'Nor a ghost you fear to stop –
Only old Miss Wickerby
   On a short cut to the shop.'

So next day we lay in wait,
   Passed a civil time of day,
Said how pleased we were she came
   Daily down our garden-way.

Suddenly her cheek it paled,
   Turned, as quick, from ice to flame.
'Tell me,' said Miss Wickerby.
   'Who spoke of me, and my name?'

'Bill the garden-boy.'
                 She sighed,
   Said, 'Of course, you could not know
How he drowned – that very pool –
   A frozen winter – long ago.'

Tom Bone

My name is Tom Bone,
I live all alone
In a deep house on Winter Street.
   Through my mud wall
   The wolf-spiders crawl
   And the mole has his beat.

On my roof of green grass
All the day footsteps pass
In the heat and the cold,
   As snug in a bed
   With my name at its head
   One great secret I hold.

Tom Bone, when the owls rise
In the drifting night skies
Do you walk round about?
  All the solemn hours through
  I lie down just like you
  And sleep the night out.

Tom Bone, as you lie there
On your pillow of hair,
What grave thoughts do you keep?
  Tom says, Nonsense and stuff!
  You'll know soon enough.
  Sleep, darling, sleep.

Out in the Desert

Out in the desert lies the sphinx
It never eats and it never drinx
Its body quite solid without any chinx
And when the sky's all purples and pinx
(As if it was painted with coloured inx)
And the sun it ever so swiftly sinx
Behind the hills in a couple of twinx
You may hear (if you're lucky) a bell that clinx
And also tolls and also tinx
And they say at the very same sound the sphinx
It sometimes smiles and it sometimes winx:

But nobody knows just what it thinx.

Fable

I was a slave on Samos, a small man
Carelessly put together; face a mask
So frightful that at first the people ran
Away from me, especially at dusk.

I was possessed, too, of a rattling tongue
That only now and then would let words pass
As they should properly be said or sung.
In general, you could say I was a mess.

One thing redeemed me. People marvelled at
The brilliance with which my speech was woven.
It was, they said, as if a toad had spat
Diamonds. And my ugliness was forgiven.

Soon I was freed, and sooner was the friend
Of kings and commoners who came a-calling.
Of my bright hoard of wit there seemed no end,
Nor of the tales that I rejoiced in telling.

But there were heads and hearts where, green and
    cold,
The seeds of envy and of hate were lying.
From our most sacred shrine, a cup of gold
Was hidden in my store, myself unknowing.

'Sacrilege! He is thief!' my accusers swore,
And to the cliffs of Delphi I was taken,
Hurled to the myrtle-scented valley floor
And on its whitest stones my body broken.

'This is the end of him and his poor fame!'
I heard them cry upon the gleaming air.
Stranger, now tell me if you know my name,
My story of the Tortoise and the Hare?'

Perhaps it's appropriate that the most famous writer of fables, known to us as Aesop, also has what are probably a great many unhistorical and legendary stories told about his life. The poem collects some of these 'facts' together: including the belief that he had a stammer. If Aesop was one person (and not, as some scholars say, merely the name given to a whole group of storytellers) it is at least fairly certain that he lived in about the sixth century BC.

The Forest of Tangle

Deep in the Forest of Tangle
The King of the Makers sat
With a faggot of stripes for the tiger
And a flitter of wings for the bat.

He'd teeth and he'd claws for the cayman
And barks for the foxes and seals,
He'd a grindstone for sharpening swordfish
And electrical charges for eels.

He'd hundreds of kangaroo-pouches
On bushes and creepers and vines,
He'd hoots for the owls, and for glow-worms
He'd goodness knows how many shines.

He'd bellows for bullfrogs in dozens
And rattles for snakes by the score,
He'd hums for the humming-birds, buzzes for bees,
And elephant trumpets galore.

He'd pectoral fins for sea-fishes
With which they might glide through the air,
He'd porcupine quills and a bevy of bills
And various furs for the bear.

But O the old King of the Makers
With tears could have filled up a bay,
For no one had come to his warehouse
These many long years and a day.

And sadly the King of the Makers
His bits and his pieces he eyed
As he sat on a rock in the midst of his stock
And he cried and he cried and he cried.
He cried and he cried and he cried and he cried,
He cried and he cried and he cried.

Mary, Mary Magdalene

Mary, Mary Magdalene
Lying on the wall,
I throw a pebble on your back.
Will it lie or fall?

Send me down for Christmas
Some stockings and some hose,
And send before the winter's end
A brand-new suit of clothes.

Mary, Mary Magdalene
Under a stony tree,
I throw a pebble on your back.
What will you send me?

I'll send you for your Christening
A woollen robe to wear,
A shiny cup from which to sup,
And a name to bear.

Mary, Mary Magdalene
Lying cool as snow,
What will you be sending me
When to school I go?

I'll send a pencil and a pen
That write both clean and neat.
And I'll send to the schoolmaster
A tongue that's kind and sweet.

Mary, Mary Magdalene
Lying in the sun,
What will you be sending me
Now I'm twenty-one?

I'll send you down a locket
As silver as your skin,
And I'll send you a lover
To fit a gold key in.

Mary, Mary Magdalene
Underneath the spray,
What will you be sending me
On my wedding-day?

I'll send you down some blossom,
Some ribbons and some lace,
And for the bride a veil to hide
The blushes on her face.

Mary, Mary Magdalene
Whiter than the swan,
Tell me what you'll send me,
Now my good man's dead and gone.

I'll send to you a single bed
On which you must lie,
And pillows bright where tears may light
That fall from your eye.

Mary, Mary Magdalene
Now nine months are done,
What will you be sending me
For my little son?

I'll send you for your baby
A lucky stone, and small,
To throw to Mary Magdalene
Lying on the wall.

On the south wall of the church of St Mary Magdalene at Launceston in
Cornwall is a granite figure of the saint. The children of the town say that
a stone lodged on her back will bring good luck.

Dream Poem

I have not seen this house before
Yet room for room I know it well:
A thudding clock upon the stair,
A mirror slanted on the wall.

A round-pane giving on the park.
Above the hearth a painted scene
Of winter huntsmen and the pack.
A table set with fruit and wine.

Here is a childhood book, long lost.
I turn its wasted pages through:
Every word I read shut fast
In a far tongue I do not know.

Out of a thinness in the air
I hear the turning of a key
And once again I turn to see
The one who will be standing there.

St Neot

St Neot, St Neot
I've heard tell
Spent his days
In a Holy Well.
Up to his neck
He was, was he,
With three little fish
For company.

St Neot sang
In water bright
The Book of Psalms
Morning to night
And then for supper
He would take
One little fish
To broil or bake.

When daylight came
St Neot would bring
Himself to swim,
Himself to sing
Where in the water
Pure and plain
Three little fish
They swam again.

The ninth-century St Neot, a famously small man, is believed to have lived in the Cornish village which bears his name. It is said that he had to stand on a stool when taking services so that the congregation could see him. Among the wonderful stained-glass windows in the church is one given by the young men of the parish in 1528, showing some of his adventures.

Who?

Who is that child I see wandering, wandering
Down by the side of the quivering stream?
Why does he seem not to hear, though I call to him?
Where does he come from, and what is his name?

Why do I see him at sunrise and sunset
Taking, in old-fashioned clothes, the same track?
Why, when he walks, does he cast not a shadow
Though the sun rises and falls at his back?

Why does the dust lie so thick on the hedgerow
By the great field where a horse pulls the plough?
Why do I see only meadows, where houses
Stand in a line by the riverside now?

Why does he move like a wraith by the water,
Soft as the thistledown on the breeze blown?
When I draw near him so that I may hear him,
Why does he say that his name is my own?

Index of First Lines